The Chronicles of Spivey

Written By

Philip R. Mills

For my wife Whatshername

Editor's Note

The following is a compilation of the
documents surrounding the life and times of
Dr. Flubdubulous, formerly Andrew J.
Anderson. While it would be impossible to
include all documents related the Spivey
incident, this collection was made with a
concerted effort at providing as much raw
information as possible to inform the
reader's opinion. This collection consists
of emails, letters, newspaper articles,
receipts, government documents and works by
Dr. Flubdubulous himself. All documents
are taken from what is now regarded as the
critical months May 2004 through November
2004.

Chapter 1

Daily Star-Home and Leisure Section D-*May 1, 2004*

Chance Encounter

It was the last few moments before I met Spivey. I didn't know just how precious those moments would be. But that is the way precious moments go. They slip away like water over a waterfall, handsome in the instant that they tumble over the edge, and for all their ethereal beauty, there's nothing you can do to prevent them from passing into history.

I wasn't watching a waterfall, one of the most depressingly sweet things you can do, just before I met Spivey. I was cutting the grass. More specifically, I was cutting the grass on a path that leads from the back of my apple orchard across an overgrown field to the woods at the back of my property.

It took exactly two passes to cut the path. One there and one back. I designed it that way. I love that efficiency. The path wasn't exactly straight however. It wound around ant hills, sticker bushes and small trees. Not so efficient.

I cut the meandering path all the way to the tree line, made a one-eighty then headed back to the apple orchard, mentally calculating all the acts necessary to take over the world. I was thinking of primarily nonviolent means. However, a violent takeover would do in a pinch, I thought as I rounded the curve around an elderberry bush and first laid eyes on Spivey. He was in the middle of the half of the path yet to be cut. I thought he was a child's toy and I instantly got angry because I had told my children to take care not to leave toys on the grounds. I hated to stop the mower, get off, then move something that shouldn't have been there in the first place.

My anger was such that I wanted to drive right over that toy and destroy it. Then it occurred to me that my children are all grown and they haven't played with toys in many years. I yanked hard on the wheel and missed Spivey by a billionth of an inch. I remember thinking that he looked like an army helmet for a three year old as I ripped by him.

I hit the brakes and brought the mower to a slamming halt. I hopped off and headed back to Spivey whom I had never laid eyes on before the moment before. He was all pulled into his shell. He looked almost innocent, all retracted in his little movable fortress.

I immediately hit the dirt. I scanned the area carefully. Spivey may have seemed like a common box turtle taking a short cut across my freshly mowed path but that is just the sort of ruse used by the best assassins in the world. Assassins of the caliber my enemies would send after me.

Most Americans have notions of animals which are the sole propriety of the media. They put all sorts of traits on to animals which are misplaced. Wolves are bad, Dolphins and Turtles are nice. Nothing could be further from the truth.

Dolphins, for example, are the bullies of the sea. Dolphins get the best press of any animal and they deserve it least. They aren't cuddly, smart, big brained distant relatives who often save sailors and entertain beach goers. They are mean, vicious water thugs who harass marine life. Dolphins drown sea turtles for fun, beat up various fish and will try to rape just about anything that moves.

Did you know that so called "Killer" whales aren't whales at all? They're big, nasty, smelly, baby whale killing, Dolphins but that's not something the pro-Dolphin media would ever tell you. You can keep the Dolphins but I'll stick with the sharks, a real fish, not a mammal parading as a fish, that makes no pretense about wanting to chew you up and eat you. Sharks may unceremoniously make a meal out of you but you won't find one hiring a PR firm or power lunching with Hollywood Execs.

And what is a turtle? Its nothing more than a land Dolphin to hear our media tell it. Five minutes with Spivey would disabuse you of all you thought you knew about turtles. He's a cold blooded back yard terrorist who is so into fighting that he carries his fortress with him. He is nature's own mobile armored fighting unit.

Once I realized this was indeed a chance encounter rather than an assassination attempt, I picked him up to look him in the eye. He has red eyes. Believe me when I tell you that a colder more penetrating stare you will not see. It was as if my soul was being skewered with salted, sharpened steel spikes.

In that instant, one of Spivey's claws shot out from his shell and touched my hand. The contact so shocked me that I dropped him. As soon as he hit the ground he made a run for it. He was in the tall grass before I could give chase. I could have dove in after him but I foolishly let him go. Mercy is wasted on the merciless. In my mind I was doing a noble thing but in Spivey's mind, as I would come to know, I was being a sucker. He was quickly planning his revenge as he slowly made his getaway.

Dr. Flubdubulous

> -----Original Message-----
From: Tom Anderson [mailto:Ufale@napkin.net]
Sent: Saturday, May 1, 2004 9:14 AM
To: Dr. Flubdubulous
Subject: Gore in 04

I think Gore has a chance in this next election if he would only run. Imagine if Gore had not had his 2000 victory taken away. A great many things would be different. I wish that you would admit to this truth.

Tom,

From: Dr. Flubdubulous [mailto:DrF@napkin.net]
Sent: Saturday, May 1, 2004 10:00 AM
To: Tom Anderson
Subject: Re: Gore in 04

Blah Blah Blah Hey, I have a suggestion, why don't you build a time machine, use it to go back to the year 1999 and give ol Al a shot of courage? You know where to get courage? You'll find it in the pharmacy next to the heterosexual pills another item which may be of interest to you.

Al had his chance and he blew it. Then Bush screwed up just as AL and everyone predicted with great detail. Yet, no part of this tragic analysis of tragedy moved Al to fight the Bush v. Gore decision so as to prevent the tragedy of Bush tragically continuing on as President.

If we get another Bush term in office this country is sunk. I think we should get a real candidate for the Democratic Party and when that person wins he/she can hire AL as Minister of I Told You So or perhaps, Secretary of I Was Right.

6

The only thing more disconcerting than your sad devotion to the man who would not win at any cost is your belief that I could be convinced of supporting said sad buffoon.

Best,

PS When you meet with Mr. Al Gore to discuss campaign strategy be sure to show him a picture of the refrigerator you bought to put in your classroom. You won't need to discuss the numerous tons of burning coal that will be necessary to keep it on 24/7 so as to secure your comfort because he already knows about it as well as all the environmental damage which will result. Don't worry about him becoming cross with you because he is after all a politician. He knows better than most how to make a deal. He'll use the same steely resolve he used when he served cake to the Communist officials who ordered the Tiananmen Square Massacre. I will concede however that on that occasion, he had the good taste to respectfully wait for the echoes from the screams of the slain to fully fade before he began to cut the cake.

```
From: Tom Anderson [mailto:Ufale@napkin.net]
Sent: Saturday, May 1, 2004 4:43 PM
To: Dr. Flubdubulous
Subject: Gore in 04
```

Angry...Angry boy.

Susquehanna Junior College

Human Resources
Glough Building
Xxxxxxxxxxxxxx
Xxxxxxxxxxxxxx

May 3, 2004

Andrew J. Anderson
XXXXXXXXX

XXXXXXXXXx
XXXXXXXXXx

Dear Mr. Anderson,

According to our records your leave of absence
due to health reasons concluded two months ago.
You have not attended your position since your
scheduled date to return to work. Our efforts
to contact you have been unsuccessful. If we
do not hear from you within 30 days from the
date of this letter your employment with
Susquehanna Junior college will be terminated.

Sincerely,

XXXXX XXXXXXXX

Director of Human Resources

c/f

_____

Dear Dr. Flubdubulous,

     I am a big fan of yours. I read your
column whenever it is in the paper but I didn't
I what you said about Dolpines. I love
Dolphines. I just thought I'd tell you your
not my favorite anymore.

Signed

XXXXXX

_____

> -----Original Message-----
From: Tom Anderson [mailto:Ufale@napkin.net]

Sent: Monday, May 3, 2004 9:14 AM
To: Dr. Flubdubulous
Subject: Spivey Column

I liked your latest column.

Tom,

From: Dr. Flubdubulous [mailto:DrF@napkin.net]
Sent: Sunday, May 3, 2004 10:00 AM
To: Tom Anderson
Subject: Re: Spivey Column

Who the hell asked ya?

Best,

_____

> -----Original Message-----
From: Dolly Anderson [mailto:kittygrl@napkin.net]
Sent: Monday, May 3, 2004 9:30 AM
To: Sue Green
Subject: Dinner

Sue,

I want to apologize to you for the way I acted
the other day. These past few months have been
very stressful for me. You know Andy hasn't
been the same since it happened. I worry about
him and the bills. I know how hard its been
for him. But that's no excuse for the way I
snapped at you when you asked and for that I am
sorry.

Dolly,

PS Could we have dinner again soon?

From: Sue Green [mailto:sgrn1959@napkin.net]
Sent: Monday, May 3, 2004 9:14 AM
To: Dolly Anderson
Subject: Re: Dinner

You don't have to apologize to ME. Everyone
has hard times. You'll pull through this I
know. Of course we'll have dinner. Just let
me know when and where.

Sue,

_____

> -----Original Message-----

From: Dr. Flubdubulous [mailto:DrF@napkin.net]
Sent: Sunday, May 3, 2004 10:00 AM
To: Tom Anderson
Subject: Re: Obituary

Today they had an interesting one. It was a 23
year old man. He drowned in a lake. It seems
he and his family were attending a religious
outing on a lake. Here's the weird part: he
drowned while swimming across a small cove at
the tip of the lake. It was about two hundred
feet across. He got about half way and started
yelling for help. Here's the even weirder
part: Someone from the gathering swam out to
him but swam back claiming that he couldn't
bring him in. Eventually the splashing died
away and his family, standing on the shore,
watched him go down. It must have been awful
for them.

All I could think of was how stupid and useless
it all was. If I had been there I could have
swam out there and pulled him out. Two hundred

10

feet is nothing. As you well know, I can swim like a fish.

This young man was a reporter for a local newspaper. He was just starting out in life. He didn't have any diseases, no bullet wounds, no blood loss, no head full of booze. Just a shitload of bad luck.

As we have discussed I usually feel a slight sense of accomplishment when I see that I have lived longer than someone, which is probably the principal reason I read the obits but I didn't feel good about this one. It was just a damn tragedy.

I cannot help but wonder: If someone had to die that day, in that small portion of lake, why couldn't it have been my brother Tom?

Best,

Daily Star-Home and Leisure Section D-*May15, 2004*

Killfests for All

Everyone got upset over remarks made by the president concerning our latest Killfest. He compared it to the Killfest which took place in Vietnam. Vietnam is always a touchy subject because it was by far our least loved Killfest.

Very often people will say that we "lost" Vietnam. Don't you believe it. When you love killfests as much as we Americans do just being there is winning. Forcing the enemy to humbly sign a "peace" treaty certainly puts the icing on the cake but it's really just a small portion of the many joys killfests bring.

You may be skeptical of my support of Killfests since my entire military career consists of me crying like a little girl in the post office while filling out my draft registration form at age 18 (Too bad they don't give out medals for being true to yourself!) But I know a winner when I see one.

Of course it's tough to choose but I think my favorite part of the Killfest cycle occurs just before the actual killing starts when everyone laments the horrors of Killfests while agreeing that they are inevitable. I think it is the purity of that belief in the inevitability of a Killfest which I admire. Its seamless texture is a thing of beauty. You can't have a Killfest without believers anymore than you can have a baloney sandwich without baloney.

After all, all Killfests, big and small are underwritten with the timeless faith in violence as a means of solving difficulties between people(s). The cause is just if you believe in it, but that in itself is nothing if you don't believe the means to obtaining justice is through doing violent harm to others.

The path to perfection winds its way along the bloody razor's edge. We advance ourselves and indeed all mankind through mass murder. Someday, in the future of course, we shall stroll the smiling shores of nirvana but only after we have taken the time and trouble to acquire the number of Killfests that warrant that honor.

When I was a younger man I couldn't accept the truths I have related here. Then, I was a pacifist. I was young and certain. Now, I am old and experienced. I have come to know the lesser virtues of the human heart and said knowledge has replaced naiveté.

The economics of human interaction demands that blood be spilled. If one fails to pay the bill on time and in proper form, the cost grows ever higher.

America became a great nation because it has always been peopled with those who would not hesitate to pay the Butcher's bill on time and, as is the case with present circumstances, before it was due. Our Western European "allies" have decided to employ a false economy and denounce our latest Killfest. They act as if they were watching a drunken Uncle at a backyard party make a pass at one of the neighbors.

Col. Paul Tibbets, the commander of the mission wherein 80,000 people were winked out of existence in less than one one-hundredth of a second, said, "I have been convinced that we saved more lives than we took," and "I viewed my mission as one to save lives." He understood the counterintuitive truth of Killfests which is: you have to kill in order to save lives. It's hard to calculate how many lives he saved when he wiped out a city but who would argue the man is not a hero?

And yes, as is often pointed out by the antikillfesters, young people make up the majority of the Butcher's bill. But death is inevitable for us all. Our youth swim in the sweet tragedy of human conflict and some do drown in it even though they may seem close to shore and thus easily saved, they do die. I can accept that because the peace and stability we purchase with their never to be lived lives is worth the cost.

Dr. Flubdubulous

```
> -----Original Message-----
From: Tom Anderson [mailto:Ufale@napkin.net]
Sent:  Thursday, May 20, 2004 1:23 PM
To: Dr. Flubdubulous  Subject: BEER KILLS!


I thought you'd get a kick out of this.


Tom
```

BELGRADE, Serbia (XXXXXX) – A 23-year old Serb was found dead and half-eaten in the bear cage of Belgrade Zoo at the weekend **during the annual beer festival.**

The man was found naked, with his clothes lying intact inside the cage. Two adult bears, Masha and Misha, had dragged the body to their feeding corner and reacted angrily when keepers tried to recover it.

"There's a good chance he was drunk. Only an idiot would jump into the bear cage," zoo director Vuk Bojovic told Reuters.

Local media reported that police found several mobile phones inside the cage, as well as bricks, stones and beer cans

```
From: Dr. Flubdubulous [mailto:DrF@napkin.net]
Sent: Friday, May 21, 2004 3:00 AM
To: Tom Anderson
Subject: Re: BEER KILLS!
```

Damn, what a way to go. I read somewhere that Bears routinely tear the skin off of their prey and when they get humans they think that the clothes are skin. I guess the moral of this story is don't mix Bears and Beer. But then I already knew that.

Best,

PS I've decided to write a new book I'm gonna call it "The Very Unauthorized Biography of Tom Anderson: Truth in the Balance." You will find it filled with so many errors, omissions and outright fabrications that it'll make the average resume look like a fountain of truth.

My Dearest Polly,

I think you should focus on your school work and not worry so much about me. Your last letter asked a great many questions I cannot answer. As to my recent decisions, all I can tell you is that I do what I can when I can.

Yes, these past few months have forced me to reevaluate a great many beliefs I've lived with most of my life but that is the way of things sometimes. You have your entire life ahead of you and college is the best way I know of for you to prepare for that life. Don't waste the opportunity worrying about me. Your mother does enough of that for ten people.

As to your question concerning the farm, it was mostly corn for cattle feed when I purchased it. I converted the one field to the orchard and let the other fields grow in. The walking paths were cut by me after several years of growth. The back field where we used to follow the rabbit tracks in the snow when you were small was sown with hay. The woods were always woods. I did very little with them except take out the dead fall from time to time.

I'm guessing from the sudden interest in the history of the farm you are feeling somewhat homesick. Don't feel bad. As much as you miss us here we miss you more.

All my love,

PS I do remember when you first went to school, actually it was a program called Head Start. You were excited to go. You bounded up onto the bus, took your seat and waved over and

over smiling as the bus pulled away. Your
mother cried like you had just left for the
gulag and we'd never see you again.

I never told you but I went to the Head
Start building and watched you from where you
couldn't see me that first day.

You did well then and you will do well now.

> -----Original Message-----
From: Dr. Flubdubulous [mailto:DrF@napkin.net]
Sent: Saturday, May 22, 2004 1:23 PM
To: Tom Anderson **Subject:** Just so you know

I just wanted to let you know that I'd just as soon kill you as
look at you.

Best,

PS This week some guy at some production company
requested some script I wrote. It is total garbage and I
should be spanked by supermodels for at least three days
for even committing such drivel to paper. Oh yeah and I
should be forced to drink a lot of beer too. Alas there is no
justice in this world. And certainly not the sweaty,
naughty, drunken justice I deserve.

From: Tom Anderson [mailto:Ufale@napkin.net]
Sent: Saturday, May 22, 2004 1:23 PM
To: Dr. Flubdubulous **Subject:** Just so you know

Message received.

Tom

> -----Original Message-----
From: Dr. Flubdubulous [mailto:DrF@napkin.net]
Sent: Thursday, May 27, 2004 3:23 AM
To: Bruce Bauries Euphoria Pictures

Subject: Query Letters

Sir,

I have been in expectation of receiving queries from you. I realize that as a producer your days are filled with meetings, power lunches, ordering assassinations, and slapping around supermodels however, I was hoping you could take a small break from those duties and send me some more queries. Thank you.

Best,
Dr. F.

From: Bruce Bauries Euphoria Pictures [mailto:bbauries@hollywood.net]
Sent: Friday, May 28, 2004 1:23 PM
To: Dr. Flubdubulous **Subject:** Re: Query Letters

Sorry no supermodels today. Dammit! I will send you the query letters today.

Your coverage on the last two scripts we sent you was excellent. Your first check should arrive any day now.

Blessings

Bruce

FALTHOR SAVINGS and
LOAN

XXXXXXXX
XXXXXXXX
XXXXXXX

Dear Mr. Andrew J. Anderson,

Our records indicate that your mortgage payment is two months overdue. We here at Falthor Savings and Loan would prefer to work with you concerning your mortgage rather than let the matter go into foreclosure. Please contact me at your earliest convenience.

Sincerely,

Philip R. Hock

Dear Sir,

　　To date, you have sent three letters enquiring about becoming a Neurosurgeon for our hospital. We do not hire surgeons but rather we extend privileges to board certified medical personnel who provide medical services in our area. Your willingness to "work for minimum wage" and your ability to "learn fast" is unfortunately not enough to qualify you to perform neurosurgery at this hospital. However if you check our website, in the human resources section, there is a frequently updated list of open positions one of which may better match your qualifications.

Sincerely,
Dr. Stillwell
Chief of Surgery

Dear Sir,

I thank you for finally responding to my letters of enquiry however, you did not answer my question as to your name. Is that your real name or did you assume it when you chose to go into medicine?

Sincerely,

Dr. Flubdubulous

PS Did I mention that I am real good at washing my hands? If you hired me as a surgeon (it doesn't have to be neurosurgery I would be willing to work as a general surgeon to start) I bet I wouldn't give any infections to any of the patients. Please consider it.

The Franks Literary Agency LLC

149 E. 45th St.

New York, NY.

Dear Dr. Flubdubulous,

I am happy to inform you that I have decided to work with you concerning your project titled "Diabetametrics, the Unreal Story of a True Superhero." Enclosed you will find a standard publishing contract. Please sign it and send it to my office. I thank you and look forward to reading your first submission.

Sincerely,

Dan Franks

The Franks Literary Agency LLC

149 E. 45th St.

New York, NY.

Dear Sir,

Enclosed is Chapter 1 of "Diabetametrics: The Unreal Story of a True Superhero." If anyone else sees this work you must kill them immediately. Do not hesitate. Do not be concerned that you might splash blood on your precious new couch. Just kill them. If they beg for mercy you are to listen politely then kill them. If the person you are about to kill looks like me, STOP. It might actually be me and killing me would make no sense since I wrote the work you are killing to protect. If the person you are about to kill looks like you, STOP. It might actually be you which would also make no sense since you have my permission to read this. Just take your time, read the chapter, enjoy it, have a glass of water and then kill without mercy anyone you have to.

Sincerely,

Dr. Flubdubulous

Diabetametrics:
The Unreal Story of a True Superhero

Written by Dr. Flubdubulous

Chapter 1

Howard Flynn's lawnmower wasn't working right. It was running fine it just wasn't cutting like it was supposed to. He couldn't understand what the problem was. It just wasn't cutting right. First it was skinning the ground on the low spots then after he adjusted the wheels it was cutting the high spots and leaving the low spots untouched.

He just stood in the driveway of his Long Island home staring at the recalcitrant mower. It didn't move. It was a push mower. He stared at it some more.

He couldn't understand how it had worked so well for years and now it wasn't working. It wasn't that he couldn't understand breakdowns. They were easy to grasp. A sudden violent rattle, a choke, then a misfire from the engine, then a sputter or two and then silence. Easy enough, but this was subtle and subtle didn't work for Howard Flynn. In fact, he had loved it when President George W. Bush said, "I don't do nuance." He got that.

Howard stood there, staring at the lawn
mower pondering the possibilities. He got as
far as the spark plug then his mind began to
wander. Why should anything break down he
wondered. It's time that does it, he decided.
It's God damned time.

He didn't want to think about time
anymore. Doing so just frustrated him. He'd
always believed that it was better to not think
about things that are frustrating and probably
unknowable.

He knelt down and grasped the front tire
nearest him and lifted the mower to look
underneath. The sweet chlorophyll perfume of
cuttings past wafted up toward him. Nothing
obvious caught his eye.

"Damn," he muttered to himself.

He leaned in for a closer inspection as if
putting his head in closer proximity to the
elusive problem would cause it to reveal itself
to him. Then he felt it. The dull ache in his
bladder telling him it was time again.

"Damn" he muttered to himself again.

Lately, it seemed, he was either drinking
something or going to the bathroom. Water in
water out, he thought. He chose to continue
staring at the underside of the mower deck. He
figured he would put his bladder on hold. It
was an interruption and Howard hated to be
interrupted no matter what the reason.
Interruptions made him angry. But then lately
everything was making him angry. He thought
about that for a moment.

He'd decided after reflecting on it that
the lawnmower problem had earned the anger he
was throwing at it but the bladder issue was
not wholly justified. He put the mower down
and rose to go to the bathroom. He was about
to turn away but started staring again despite
the pressure he was now feeling in his bladder
which had miraculously doubled since he had
made the decision to heed the call. It was as
if he had started the launch sequence and all

things were preparing to go which made aborting the mission that much more painful.

Howard continued to stare at the mower however his thoughts were few. It was as if his mind was on the verge of a profound thought. Not an epiphany, just a really good thought. But then it delivered nothing. Somehow, Howard thought that if he waited a little more the time spent would be rewarded. Like some senior citizen patiently pumping quarters into a slot machine with the firm faith the next one will yield the jackpot.

It didn't happen. In fact very little crossed the vast blank screen in his head till his wife Lolly opened the door and called to him.

"What are you doing?" she asked.

Howard could feel the anger build in him instantly. She was interrupting him. And she was interrupting with a stupid question to boot.

His anger subsided when he looked up to answer her. She was standing on the stoop half out the front door. She was wearing a housecoat which made her appear to him as a wife from the 1950's. The juxtaposition of her now with the way she looked when he met her freshman year in college made for a surreal moment in his sluggish brain.

Besides it was hard for him to ever stay angry with Lolly. He truly loved her. He also decided that his anger at this point was not justified because he couldn't remember what he was angry about. That, he thought, was strange and not very much like him at all.

"I'm working on the mower"

"Oh, I wasn't sure because it looked like you were just standing there staring at it" she said smiling.

"Well despite how it looks I am working on the mower" he said his anger returning a little.

"Oh, I see you're using your psychic powers to fix the mower. I'm sorry to have interrupted you oh great one"

She turned and went back into the house. Howard stared at the screen door as it slowly closed. He couldn't take his eyes off of it. It was as if it would be painful to alter his gaze. He held his eyes on it even though he could hear someone walking up behind him.

"Whatcha looking at Howie?"

It was Bruce from across the street. Howard hated to be called Howie and he didn't want to be interrupted again. His bladder pulsed. It had to be holding a gallon he thought. He finally broke his gaze and turned.

"Hey Bruce"

"Howie, what's the deal with the mower?"

"I'm not sure. It's not cutting the lawn right."

Bruce furrowed his brow and looked down at the idle mower. Howard smiled inwardly because he knew that to Bruce, lawnmowers were either on or off. The quality of the cut was not something Bruce would concern himself with. He'd been living across the street for the past ten years and Howard doubted that Bruce had ever so much as sharpened his mower blade.

Otherwise Bruce's house was kept clean and loud. Everything about it was loud from the bright red paint to the radio which always seemed to be on. The flowerboxes under the front windows were painted with a high gloss white that made them seem neon when the sun hit them directly.

"Looks cut to me," he said sweeping the lawn with his eyes.

"It is cutting but it's skinning in some places and leaving ribbons in other places," Howard said, still looking at the mower.

"Gee Howie, sounds serious," he mocked.

"Sounds like sarcasm Bruce."

"Hi Bruce," Lolly called from the door.

She had returned while they were speaking and although the unexpected volume of her voice made Howard's nerves jump, he still did not look up from the mower. He felt them both staring at him. He felt his bladder squeeze again. He realized there was nothing emanating from his thought centers. It was time to go to the bathroom for a break.

"Excuse me," was all he said as he walked up the stoop, passed Lolly and entered the house. He could hear Lolly saying something to Bruce but none of it coalesced into any meaning. It was as if she were speaking a foreign language. Her voice grew fainter as he moved toward the bathroom.

> -----Original Message-----
From: Dr. Flubdubulous [mailto:DrF@napkin.net]
Sent: Sunday, May 28, 2004 4:33 AM
To: Bruce Bauries Euphoria Pictures **Subject:** Query Letters

I got the letters and I have already requested two scripts from among them. Thanks.

Best,

Dr. F.

PS Idea for a cable television channel: The Bikini Channel. It would feature gorgeous women in bikinis 24/7. I see, "Bikini Detective"-She solves crimes which occur on fabulous beaches of the world, "Bikini Tomorrow"- A show about a ordinary girl who gains psychic powers when she wears a bikini and she solves murders before they happen (could be some constitutional problems there but you fix that in post production with some good writers), "American Bikini"-a reality based show about girls and their bikinis, "Spring Break"-Shot like 24, each hour show represents a real hour of spring break (could take three seasons to film one Spring Break), "Bikini Biologist"-she travels the world with her crack team of bikini clad scientists and helps fix environmental damage, remove dolphins from tuna nets and so on. If beauty is truth, then this channel will be jiggling truth all over the place. I'd watch it.

CHAPTER 2

Daily Star-Home and Leisure Section D-*May 29, 2004*

God Thoughts

This morning it occurred to me that I might be God. I know what you're thinking, 'Willie Nelson is God.' I believed that for a long time too but now I am beginning to see things differently. I was harvesting plums from one of my plum trees when it occurred to me that I created life from lifelessness. Then it started to rain because I left one of my motorcycles outside the garage (a situation which brings on a rain storm one hundred percent of the time). So then it became clear to me that I can create life and command the heavens to rain. Isn't that what a God does?

Granted, my religious training was far from complete as a child and to this day I have no idea what religion my parents were, although I would guess it's the one that worships television and requires parents to yell at their children a lot.

Of course being God has tremendous responsibilities which, if my suspicions were correct, I had to consider. Divinity begets obligation. You better believe that after two quick six packs of beer I got right to the thinking.

While I was wrestling with the problems of the universe, holding it all in the subtle contempt allowed only to supreme beings, I read something by a philosopher brainiac that answered all questions.

This guy figured out mathematically (every philosopher's strong point) that there is a twenty percent chance we are, in fact, living in a virtual world set up by post-humans. According to him, we're not even real, just part of one hellaciously big computer program.

I figure there's a fifty percent chance he's seventy five percent correct so I put it together. Willie Nelson isn't God, he's the Prime Designer. We live in HIS virtual world.

Be honest, if you were the Prime Designer and therefore could make reality in your virtual world whatever you choose, wouldn't you live the life Willie has?

I know it all sounds fantastic but I quickly realized that my skepticism and yours has been written into the program. Transcending the programming is a task not easily accomplished.

It's all so deceptively simple and the evidence is in all the imperfections around us. Would we have tragedy, light beer, cancer, cellulite and guidance counselors if our universe was in fact created by a perfect God?

I should be up front and tell you that I was always a bit skeptical about the standard cosmology which my parents dutifully beat into me as a child. The one where we were all part of an unknowable plan created by a God that looked like a not so jolly version of Santa Clause. It seemed to me, in that version, the universe was no more than God's personal petting zoo.

I have since learned many differing cosmologies but I don't have much respect for any religion or philosophy that isn't endorsed by the mainstream media or backed up by large quantities of violent people threatening violence if you don't respect their version of the facts.

But still, the brainiac philosopher was pretty sure of himself.

Of course having such knowledge does not put a gentleman of fortune such as me in a comfortable position. I have to weigh my obligation to the truth against my burning hatred for all people. In the end I reasoned that since I am neither a God nor even the Prime Designer I could do as I pleased and because it was something no one, not even Willie, would expect, I chose to serve my alleged responsibility to humanity.

There's only one problem. The philosopher brainiac thinks that if everyone in the virtual world were to figure out they were in a virtual world they would start to rework their reality towards their tastes which would probably cause the great computer to crash. Now you know more than you should.

Dr. Flubdubulous

> -----Original Message-----

From: Rev. Hummel [mailto:rhummel@ether.net]
Sent: Monday, May 31, 2004 8:00 AM
To: Dr. Flubdubulous

Subject: Newspaper Column

Dear Sir,

I took great offense at your last newspaper column.
Your blasphemy is intolerable and I intend to seek
legal remedy to keep you from ever printing such
filth again. Meanwhile I shall pray for your
eternal soul and hope that Jesus enters your heart
and stops you from writing anymore blasphemous
columns.

Sincerely,
Reverend Hummel
Sacred Church of the Divine Jesus

From: Dr. Flubdubulous [mailto:rhummel@ether.net]
Sent: Monday, May 31, 2004 10:00 AM
To: Rev. Hummel
Subject: Re: Newspaper Column

Dear Sir,

Your threats concerning my mission to bring
truth to a weary world have no place in
civility. If shame was a concept not unknown
to you I would not have to tell you the
significance of my work to posterity nor would
it be necessary for me to point out to you that
I have legal representation too. My lawyer, a
man you routinely wronged and insulted
throughout your chestnut existence, is an
expert at handling spurious lawsuits. He'll go
through you and your subpoenas like Jell-O
through a trash compacter.

Very Sincerely,
Dr. Flubdubulous

_____

> -----Original Message-----

DELETED FOR REASONS UNKNOWN

From: Dr. Flubdubulous [mailto:DrF@napkin.net]
Sent: Tuesday, June 1, 2004 3:00 AM
To: Tom Anderson
Subject: RE: nyaa nyaa

Regarding the article you sent, "Research Finds
Firstborns Gain the Higher I.Q." I found it
interesting. It put me in mind of another
study that I read several months ago which
concluded that the first born will inevitably
suffer from sexual dysfunction. I also
remember reading somewhere that the first born
male is usually a sissy-Mary-momma's-boy who
couldn't get a date at a Slut Convention. But
what do scientists know?
Best,

PS

If you want to compare IQ's mine has been
clocked as a solid 78. That's SOLID!

FALTHOR SAVINGS and LOAN

XXXXXXXX
XXXXXXXX
XXXXXXX

Dear Mr. Andrew J. Anderson,

Our records indicate that your mortgage payment is three months
overdue. We here at Falthor Savings and Loan would prefer to
work with you concerning your mortgage rather than let the

matter go into foreclosure. Please contact me at your earliest convenience.

Sincerely,

Philip R. Hock

———————————————————

My Dearest Polly,

    To answer your question, I only knew one of my grandparents. My paternal grandfather. He died when I was about your age.

    My grandfather was quite a person. Like the rest of his generation he achieved so much and thought so little of his accomplishments. That is not to say he wasn't proud of them but he just never thought that they were a big deal.

    The thing I most admired about my grandfather was that he lived his dreams. He had small dreams to be sure but he lived them nevertheless. I, on the other hand didn't have a clue as to what I wanted when I was a young man.

    When my grandfather was a kid he knew what he wanted but the war came along and he was thrust into it. He had joined "early" as he called it. A nice way of saying he joined before he was drafted. It was just his manner of downplaying the act of volunteering to go.

    He landed in North Africa and was engaged in nearly every big battle from that point till the end of the war. Hard to believe such a gentle man would be part of such violence. And just as mysterious was his reluctance to take credit for his accomplishments.

31

Once, when I was about five years old, he was telling me about the war and how he was a soldier. I asked him with the openness only a child of five can have, if he'd killed Germans during the war? He said in his quiet voice, "oh yes" paused for a moment as if respect demanded a moment of reflection on such a matter, then began talking again right at the point I had interrupted him with my question.

I found out later that he killed his first German soldier by accident. It was in North Africa and it was one of his first combats. The two armies had met up and were at the stage of combat when everyone scrambles for cover and starts to maneuver independently. Before the officers and sergeants take stock and start organizing the killing.

He was running down a gully. The gully provided cover and he thought he was heading toward his squad. He was running with his rifle leveled chest high. The rifle had an eighteen inch bayonet on the end. The gully made a 90 degree right turn. As he approached the turn a German soldier about his age ran around the corner and ran right into his razor sharp bayonet. The young German soldier was as shocked as he was that it had happened. The difference of course was that the young German Soldier had only seconds to ponder the magnitude of what had just happened and my grandfather would have a lifetime to think about it.

I often wondered about that death. Why did that gully have a 90 degree turn? Perhaps that turn was the result of a huge rock having been laid there millions of years before that German soldier was born. The immovable rock caused the water run off in that area to turn and gouge out a gully with a blind spot. After all, the iceberg hit by the Titanic was formed from snow that had fallen ten thousand years before that noble ship sailed.

When that German boy was born his parents

32

were probably happy and had no idea the life they'd just witnessed start would be ended so soon and so harshly. They didn't know, or would ever know, the young man who would kill their young man.

One day during the German boy's life, probably while he was in High School, a factory in the U.S., unbeknownst to him, was manufacturing the very bayonet that would one day pass through his diaphragm and lower heart. It was polished and carefully laid in a box for shipment. And the man who would one day wield that weapon was probably working on very similar algebra problems in *his* high school.

As it was described to me, a look of shock and fear registered for a moment on the young German soldier's face then the look drained away with his life. No sweetheart, no wife, no children, no growing older. He simply had no life.

Granted there were a great many things that contributed to the meeting of those two young men that day. Not the least of which was the rise of Nazism. But man, it makes you think.

If the situation had been the reverse, I may never have been born. A rock falls into a place long before humans are around to invent war and bayonets, and yet it affects the outcome of a chance encounter.

I hope this information helps you with your anthropology class. If you need any additional information about the family I will gladly provide it for you and I promise not to go on so.

All my love

-----Original Message-----

From: Tom Anderson [mailto:Ufale@napkin.net]
Sent: Thursday, June 3, 2004 4:28 PM

To: Dr. Flubdubulous

Subject: Re: Why Gore Should Run - And How He Can Win

Your boy from New Mexico supported a Republican against the wishes of his party. A Republican!! Also, he has a fatal problem with women. He sexually harasses them, and there are several waiting in the wings should his campaign become successful...it won't. GORE in 2004!!!

From: Dr. Flubdubulous [mailto:DrF@napkin.net]
Sent: Friday, June 4, 2007 1:12 AM
To: Tom Anderson
Subject: Why Gore Should Run - And How He Can Win

How typical. Tom starts the attack machine the second he feels threatened by democracy. Maybe what you call sexual harassment is what others may refer to as unrequited love, the saddest, sweetest, and most difficult love to have to deal with. Instead of showing concern for Mr. Richardson's plight, you want to show him the door. How pitiable is it that you could have so little pity for a man who, very much like yourself, has suffered a great deal of rejection from women?

Richardson supported a Republican so that he could look bipartisan. A ham-handed attempt to be sure but not nearly comparable to Gore glad handing with the Chinese Communist Party honchos who ordered up the Tiananmen Square massacre.

Al had his day in court and he had his chance. He blew it! We don't need him on the ticket polling people to see which color suit he should wear.

34

Best,

_____

> -----Original Message-----
From: Rev. Hummel [mailto: rhummel@ether.net]
Sent: Friday June 4, 2004 8:00 AM
To: Dr. Flubdubulous
Subject: Your Recent Letter

Dear Sir,

Your recent letter to me as well as the

blasphemous sentiments you routinely include in

your column clearly indicate that you are a man

without morals or honor. You can be assured

that I shall do all that is within my powers to

stop your assault on decency. I shall pray for

your eternal soul.

Sincerely,
Reverend Hummel
Sacred Church of the Divine Jesus

From: Dr. Flubdubulous [mailto: rhummel@ether.net]
Sent: Friday, June 4, 2004 3:00 PM
To: Rev. Hummel
Subject: Newspaper Column

Dear Sir,

I was interested to receive your email today
because as it happens, I had a dream about you
last night. It's true! In my dream, I was
floating above a huge water tank in a room

without walls. You were at the center of the water tank lying on the water with your arms outstretched in the way our lord and savior Jesus was posed on the cross. Circling you in the water was a pod of dolphins. You had a look of absolute serenity on your face. It was as if you had been touched by the grace of heaven and you were basking in its glorious wonderment. Then, all at once, the Dolphins stopped their forward motion and turned to you. They approached you and one gently nuzzled your right hand. After a most tender moment, the water began to bubble and roil and the Dolphins attacked you. When they brought you up for air they began raping you. Each one raping you in turn. Raping, raping, raping, over and over. It was hour after hour of you screaming, howling, begging them to stop.

I'm not sure what the dream meant, but man, it makes you think.

Very Sincerely,

Dr. Flubdubulous

SPIVEY MUST DIE

All my life I have played a game in my head. The game is essentially this: I try to determine what is/was the best moment of my life and which is/was the worst. Naturally, this is an exceedingly difficult task as the list of experiences is constantly being added to. However there is a further complication which is that the appraisal of outcomes of past events are constantly changing also.

One might think of one's wedding day as the best day of one's life until that other day. The day six years later when one is signing the divorce papers in the clammy office of a clammy lawyer. Just as good moments become bad moments the reverse is true. One might be upset at being fired and consider that a bad moment until the events which stem from that moment end up in more favorable terms.

I believe one could determine just how chaotic their life is/was by the number of reversals in this game. That is, the number of times one has to reassign the designation of particular chosen moments. I've semi-seriously dubbed this the K-factor and I have never attempted the mathematics to make this into a scaled score. I suspect to do so one would have to turn reality inside out just for openers.

It follows however that if one had a low K-factor then one would be more certain of events. A low K-factor individual is pretty good at calling them when they happen as opposed to someone like myself who has had so many reversals, and thus a high K-factor, that I'm always in doubt. Us high K-factor types know better than to categorize any moment with mortar.

Despite my being in the camp of the very uncertain I've come to believe that my first meeting with Spivey was one of, if not *the* worst, moments of my life. I started to believe, as it happens, just the other day.

It was late afternoon and the heat of the day was being pushed away by a gentle breeze from the east. I decided that now might be a good time to cut some grass. I crossed the yard slowly taking in the beauty of the day. The greens and blues mixed with the sounds of birds chirping gathered in my mind as an impressionist masterpiece. I was so lost in the moment that I didn't notice anything wrong until I was only a few feet from the open shed door.

For one thing, that door was always kept closed, but I could also see that my lawnmower was sitting at a strange angle. I immediately stepped to my right two steps to take it in from another angle. It was still not right. I approached it cautiously. I instantly thought of explosives but then I realized that any assassin motivated to do me in with explosives wouldn't be stupid enough to change the appearance of the vehicle to tip me off and he would have remembered to leave the door as he'd found it.

It was the left rear tire. It was flat. I exhaled and let the tension of the past moment drain away as I stepped up to find what had caused the flat. The tension returned immediately in the next moment when I found the cause.

Along the lower part of the tire, on the side wall just above the tread, were four, half inch long slashes. Curiously, they weren't even in length but they were even in distance from each other. I couldn't decide what could cause such a wound to a turf tire. As I stared at the deadened tire the thought coalesced in my mind. It was from a claw. More specifically the rear claw of a box turtle. Even more specifically, it was Spivey's claw!

I knew then without regard to K-factor or any other measurement known to existence that my chance encounter with Spivey two weeks before was a candidate for the worst moment in my life. I also knew that nothing was going to change that.

He had deliberately slashed that tire. He was sending me a message. It wasn't as flashy as a horse head in my bed but it was as determined. He was sending me a reptilian message. I got it loud and clear.

I could have run. I could have packed up, sold the house and lit out for parts unknown and it is likely I would never see or hear from Spivey ever again. But some threats are hard to run from.

It also occurred to me that if I were to stand my ground I could change a potential "worst" moment into a "greatest" moment. I could, after a lifetime of being pushed around by fate, make my own destiny. I could become master of all that makes moments good or bad, best or worst, and all I would need was the courage to do it.

In that instant my thoughts coalesced into one determination. A determination that was as clear to me as those irreparable tears in the innocent sidewall of that lone deflated rear tire on my beloved lawnmower. Spivey must die!

Dr. Flubdubulous

Evangelical Hospital

June 15, 2004

Dr. Flubdubulous
XXXXXXXXXXXX
XXXX XX XXXXX

Dear Doctor Flubdubulous,

I would like to thank you for inquiring about becoming a Neurosurgeon with our Hospital. We regret we are unable to offer you a position at this time.

We will be happy to keep your resume in our active file for one year, and will contact you should an appropriate position become available.

Once again, thank you for considering Evangelical Hospital as a prospective employer, and good luck in your job search!

Sincerely,

Bonnie Kearns

Hiring and Training Specialist

BB/cz

> -----Original Message-----

From: Dr. Flubdubulous [mailto: Ufale@napkin.net]
Sent: Monday, June 14, 2004 8:00 AM
To: Tom Anderson
Subject: Movie Idear

Do you recall when I was a school bus driver? I don't know if you remember this but there was this cute little girl on my bus who was murdered. She snuck out of the house to meet with her boyfriend. No one knows what happened but she was found in the reeds of that little park down by that place you and Brandon rented that year. She had been strangled. The next day the boyfriend admitted that he'd killed her. It was an absolute tragedy.

What about a movie about the bus driver? In this scenario he never forgets what happened (in this film it is an unsolved crime). Then the bus driver dies and through some sort of cosmic device he is given the opportunity to go back in time and correct one wrong. He chooses the night of the murder. He gets there and finds out that it was his brother TOM who committed that heinous crime all those years ago.

I guess the only questions one need ask for this idea are, how much would it take to produce this film? And why'd you strangle that innocent little girl Tom?

Best,

From: Tom Anderson [mailto: DrF@napkin.net]
Sent: Monday, June 14, 2004 8:00 AM
To: Dr. Flubdubulous
Subject: Movie Idear

You have the opportunity to go back in time and fix any of the many wrongs of the past and the best you can come up with is the murder of one girl? Why don't you go back and prevent a war or something as big?

Tom,

Dr. Flubdubulous replied:

What? You fix that stuff in editing.

I suppose you would rather keep her dead huh? Your
response indicates to me that I'm on to something.

Best,

_____

My dearest Polly,

     Mother is fine and so am I. Your concerns
about me although touching and welcomed, are
unwarranted. Despite appearances I can assure
you I am the same heroic father you've come to
know with awe and respect.
     As to your question concerning my last
column I shall, with your indulgence, answer it
indirectly by telling you my all time second
greatest moment and then tell you my all time
greatest moment.
     My second greatest moment occurred when
you were about five years old. It was a day in
early September. A chilling wind came down
from the north furiously replacing the last of
the late summer heat. The sky was filled with
puffy, bright white clouds cruising slowly.
     I cannot recall exactly what I was doing
when I realized that you were no longer playing
in the side yard by the drive way. I
immediately began to look for you. I headed for
the front of the house. As I rounded the
corner I saw you standing on the porch.
     You were standing on the very edge of the
side that faces the north. You were faced away
from me so you did not see me edging up on you
at an oblique angle.
     You stood there with your arms
outstretched in front of you with your palms
tilted upward. The wind was blowing your long
hair straight back. In that pose you looked

like a pagan statue. A goddess of the winds calling upon them to bring on autumn.

In my mind's eye I can still see you standing there smiling, the sun sparkling in the auburn highlights of your hair, tossed by the gusting wind. You closed your eyes and tilted your head back ever so slightly taking in the pure joy of the moment. You pulled your arms in to your body and crossed them on your chest as if you were hugging the wind itself then you shuddered, your smile widening.

That most beautiful moment ended and you turned to see me standing on the lawn watching you. You waved and ran to me.

That was the most beautiful thing I have ever seen or would ever see. That moment, coupled with your other beauties, confirmed for me that my best, greatest day was when you were born. Game Over.

All my love

PS I also decided shortly after the aforementioned story that if I ever wrote a story about raising you I would title it "Embracing the Wind."

> -----Original Message-----
From: Dr. Flubdubulous [mailto:DrF@napkin.net]
Sent: Wednesday, June 16, 2004 1:23 AM
To: Tom Anderson **Subject:** World Demands

Last night I had a dream. Not the sort of dream a great man such as Martin Luther King spoke of. This dream was quite the opposite. Whereas he dreamt of lofty human achievement my dream dealt with the lesser virtues of the human heart. Mine was about power, control, greed and avarice on a scale heretofore unparalleled.

I dreamt that I had invented a weapon of mass destruction that could destroy all life on earth in one one-hundredth of a second. The future of human kind was placed on my whim.

It was an ironically small device. Perhaps it was just the detonator, I don't know but it was the size of a graphing calculator. It had a rather uninspired design. It was gray with a single red button in the center. No turnkey, no cover, no safeties. Just a button.

I was, I'm ashamed to say, actually considering pushing the damn thing and ending all existence. I woke up sweating. That is a heavy concept to be sure but the real kicker was just how real the dream seemed. It was so clear and so filled with detail that I started to wonder if I hadn't just seen the future.

One can never know the future and basing one's behavior on dreams may be silly however, I sure as hell don't want to be caught flat footed should the aforementioned doomsday device actually come to be. Therefore I have developed a preliminary set of demands (see below) which I shall place on the peoples of earth. Their compliance with those demands may influence my decision as to their fate.

Best,

1. Hawaiian Shirts will henceforth be considered formal attire.

2. No more plastic beer bottles. Ever!

3. No more photographs of Michael Jackson.

4. No more left handed guitars. (They just confuse the hell out of everyone!)

5. End to the myth that women like sex. (We all know they don't and it's time we set the record straight.)

6. No more Vampire movies. Ever!

7. The word tragedy shall henceforth be spelled with a 'j' thusly, "trajedy"

8. No Tandem bicycles.

9. If the Boston Red Sox win the World Series the accomplishment, or miracle if you will, shall not be spoken about by anyone anywhere after one day has passed from the time they were declared winners.

10. All time zones shall keep the same time. (The way it is now is just confusing.)

PS This list is subject to change at my desire.

———————————————————————

The Gauntlet Thrown Down

As many of you who regularly read this column know my foe Spivey viciously slashed the tire on my lawnmower as a declaration of war. What I didn't know then was that his evil mind had already set its crazed imagination on the task of bringing about my destruction.

Spivey, the vicious brute, that reptilian rapscallion, centered his whole being on his desire to rid me of my life. His genius chose an elementary design for my elimination and I, like a complete fool, completely underestimated my enemy.

Make no mistake about it, this tete te' between me and Spivey has been playing out for eons. Your school books, and the media, have told you repeatedly that the dinosaurs became extinct but that is a falsehood. The dinosaurs, out of necessity, had to suspend their war with mammals and became birds. They are waiting for the right moment to strike back.

The most stubborn of the dinosaurs, the hardcore core are the reptiles you see lurking in the shadows. Their hatred for mammals is so great that they refused to hide as birds and chose instead to continue the fight albeit under reduced circumstances. They hold in the very center of their Paleozoic brains, the memory of all mammals being no bigger than mice along with a scorching desire to conquer.

I learned of the aforementioned and the disposition of my adversary the hard way, as they say, when I was walking to the back field on my property. The back field is separated from the rest of the property by a strip of woods that lays across its entirety and is twenty five meters deep. There happens to be one path into the back field that cuts through said woods. Only one. The path is just wide enough for a small tractor to make use of it.

Spivey was well aware that I would have to travel that twenty five meter stretch of path sooner or later. He also knew that stepping from the bright lit field into the darkly shaded path would inhibit my vision briefly. Armed with those two factoids he set to work.

I wandered through the field to the entrance of the path. I innocently stepped into the cool darkness of the shaded path when something caught at my foot and I lost my balance. I instinctively reached out with both my arms in a failed attempt to regain my balance. My right arm brushed against an overhanging branch. I snatched it desperately. It held just long enough to twist my body to the right. The branch broke and I went down. Right next to my eye, where I landed, was a sharpened stick standing upright. About eight inches of the stick was above ground and the end had been gnawed to a perfect point. If not for my brief hold on the overhanging branch, I would have landed on that death stick with my right eye.

It took a moment for me to recover from my fall and in that time I heard something scratching around. Then I heard it head for cover. I scrambled to my feet but it was gone. The only thing left behind were scratchings in the dirt near where I had tripped. I stared at the design in the dirt. I moved to look at them from another angle.

Finally, my subconscious mind broke through to my conscious and screamed "SPIVEY!" That is what was scratched there for me to read. I don't know if it was a threat or a curse or his name. A reptile thinks on several levels and for all I know it could be all three. I chose to see it as his calling card.

The enemy has a name and he's thrown down the gauntlet. There was no going back from this act. We were in the end game. I rushed back to the house to prepare.

Dr. Flubdubulous

From: Tom Anderson [mailto:Ufale@napkin.net]
Sent: Friday, June 18, 2004 4:25 PM
To: Dr. Flubdubulous   **Subject:** Re: World Demands

Your list of demands all seem reasonable but the thought of you with a weapon of mass destruction is frightening. Never has science gone so wrong. Hopefully the future will prove your dream was just the fiction of a sad jumbled mind.

Tom

> -----Original Message-----

Bruce Bauries Euphoria Pictures
[mailto:bbauries@hollywood.net]

We have received your coverage for "The Ladder." We agree with your opinion of this work. It is as you say "a lifeless and forced morality tale of being career minded," however, we would appreciate it if you could give notes on the script as the author is involved in a financing deal. Well, you know the rest.

B.

PS I shall have to check with our accountant as to why you have not received a check from us. I'll get back to you on that.

From: Dr. Flubdubulous [mailto:DrF@napkin.net]
Sent: Sunday, June 20, 2004 1:23 AM
To: Bruce Bauries Subject: "The Ladder"

I shall get to the notes right away.

"The Ladder" reminds me of a real story about a real guy that occurred when I was about 19 years old. This man worked hard as an engineer for the Grumman Corporation (a big employer on Long Island in those days) for many years and did well. Finally, he got the nod and was promoted to a senior management position which put him in a whole other realm. He had arrived. He had achieved economic success, status and a glorious, well earned, pat on the back. Flush with good fortune, bad fortune came looking for him. Four days after his promotion, on a crisp fall day, he decided to clean the gutters of his large house. Maybe the very things that drove him to such success were the same things that induced him to do a chore he could have afforded to pay anyone to do for him. I want to make a movie about what was going through that guy's head while he made that fatal fall.

Best,

Dr. F.

From: Tom Anderson [mailto:Ufale@napkin.net]

Sent: Sunday, June 20, 2004 10:33 AM
To: Dr. Flubdubulous

Subject: Deplorable – Disgusting – Disgraceful

Did you hear about how Major league baseball is ordering all teams to wear special spring training hats? Does it help performance? Increase training? Improve safety? NO! They just want to sell more hats. Now people who already own baseball hats can run out to buy these objects that perform the exact same function.

As I drove by Yankee stadium on Wednesday, I saw the preparations for building the new ball park. I think I now know how people from Brooklyn felt when the Dodgers left. Oh well, baseball has just kept pace with the rest of our culture. (Soon, we will have to look up to see what used to be called the bottom.) You can whore yourself out by wolfing down hot dogs in the new "Yankee Stadium," but you can do it without me. I will be at Fenway park. At least those people respect history.

Faithfully submitted, Douglas C. Neidermeyer (sssssssssss)

PS I just wanted you to know that I am back, and my operation is up and running. I am now available to distribute my inane observations and unsolicited (and equally inane) opinions. Should Your Highness be in need of such drivel, contact me.

From: Dr. Flubdubulous [mailto:DrF@napkin.net]

Sent: Sunday, June 20, 2004 6:30 PM
To: Tom Anderson

Subject: THE RETURN

So now it has come to this? I can see how the Civil War came to be Brother agin Brother. You would eschew any Yankee stadium to park your heartless carcass in FENWAY! This sort of blasphemy not only shocks the senses but justifies use of the epithet, among others, traitor. I didn't say anything when you bought a wine rack, I didn't say anything when you married a non-American woman and I didn't say anything when made all those trips to Europe but this goes too far. I've decided to place you below Brandon and Steve on the list.

Best,

PS I agree that the training camp hat is on the same line as the Vulcan Medal of Freedom. I think we could improve the lives of all Americans if we put a bounty out on all marketers and closed all college marketing programs. I doubt if we eliminated the scourge of marketing that people would stop buying things and thereby cause the economy to collapse.

PPS There is something more sinister about the reworking of Yankee stadium. They are remaking it to better serve the wealthy, e.g. permit them to view the games in luxury and at a comfortable distance from the workers who paid for the stadium. There's something about the whole scene that's Romanesque. The higher the tower is built the more it sways in the wind.

PPPS Me wolfing down hot dogs in a baseball park IS respecting history. The only greater respect I could bestow history would be watching you get drunk on overpriced beer paid for by me.

> -----Original Message-----
From: Bruce Bauries Euphoria Pictures
[mailto:bbauries@hollywood.net]
Sent: Monday, June 22, 2004 1:23 PM
To: Dr. Flubdubulous Subject: Script

I've attached a script titled, "Blood, Death and Sky" that just came to us. Give it a look-see and let us know what you think.

Blessings

Bruce

> -----Original Message-----
From: Dr. Flubdubulous [mailto:Ufale@napkin.net]
Sent: Monday, June 22, 2004 2:00 PM
To: Tom Anderson
Subject: Book

I've started work on my first novel. You want to know what it is about? I'll bet you do. I'll give you a hint. It's titled: "The Case Against My Brother Tom." It'll be a brilliant, illuminating, testament to truth. I'm going to prove to the world that all the things they thought they knew about Tom Anderson was completely false.

Best,

From: Tom Anderson [mailto: DrF@napkin.net]
Sent: Monday, June 22, 2004 8:00 PM
To: Dr. Flubdubulous
Subject: Book

Bring it on.

Tom,

REDEMPTION
By Dr. Flubdubulous

PART 1

Command Ship Reach (C.S. 401k)

Admiral Zach Harmon stood in front of the wall sized view port looking out at his fleet floating above the Kardon home world. The fleet stretched out, it's outer edges blending with the stars in the distance. He stood with his hands clasped behind his back, the very model of the stoic senior officer. Tall and lean in his dark green uniform with its white trim and canary yellow piping he would inspire even the lowliest soldier in the Star Force. He looked better than he felt.

He felt heavy. It was as if someone had turned up the gravity in his ready room. He was thinking about the impending battle of course but he was also thinking about the men and women working on those ships preparing for it. He thought of their efforts and their plans for the future. A future that for many of them wouldn't happen. How many of them had been lost since the war began?

He stood motionless on the wide platform in front of the view port. The only light in the room came streaming in from the scene outside. Heavy shadows fell across the sparsely decorated room. He didn't hear the door open.

"Sir?"

It was Ensign Pleat. Pleat was probably the oldest Ensign in the Space Force. He'd been recalled to service when the loses mounted.

Zach recognized the voice and did not turn from the view port when he acknowledged Pleat.

"What is it?" he asked without emotion.

"Sir, I know you ordered that you not be disturbed but . . ."

"But what?"

"Captain Valentine has requested to see you Sir. He says it is most important."

Zach turned his gaze from the view port to Pleat. "Didn't I warn that any interruptions and I would have you executed?"

"Ah Yes Sir, but Captain Valentine said it was urgent and I believe he is your oldest advisor."

Zach considered it for a moment then said, "Very well, send him in then have yourself executed."

"Yes Sir."

He turned back to the view port as Pleat turned to leave.

"Ensign."

"Sir?"

"Cancel your execution, I've sent enough letters home this cycle."

"Yes Sir."

Valentine stepped into the room the instant that Pleat stepped out. He wore the black on black uniform of the Suh-vak, the intelligence arm of the Space Force. He bounced up the four steps to the platform in front of the opulent viewport, the kind, he noted, that were only to be found on command ships.

He approached and saluted crisply, waited to be recognized. Valentine was slightly shorter than the Admiral. He had an athletic build and unlike any members of the Suh-vak, he had a tendency to smile.

Zach still looking at the fleet raised his arm in a half hearted return salute. Valentine dropped his salute and peered out the view port trying to discern what exactly had the Admiral's attention. He waited a beat and turned back towards Zach.

"I see you took Pleat with you to your new command."

Zach said nothing.

"You're thinking about the battle aren't you? You haven't changed a bit. You used to get that same look on your face before a big test at the academy. I remember-"

"You talk a lot. I thought intelligence officers were supposed to be listeners," Zach said flatly.

"I don't' always talk. Sometimes I hear things," Valentine said his smile fading.

Zach turned to him taking his eyes off the fleet for the first time since the conversation began. Valentine could see he had caught the Admiral's interest with that last remark.

"Like what?"

"Like this glorious war fleet of yours may be flying into a great big trap."

"This whole war has been a trap," Zach said more to himself than Valentine as he turned back to look out at the fleet and the space beyond.

"Zach you'd better take this serious," Valentine said his voice changing, more serious now. "There are many who have already gone to the other side because they don't believe we can win. They don't think this fleet has a chance even if it is commanded by the youngest Admiral in the history of the Space Force."

Zach turned and with a slight smile said, "Well, to be fair, there were a lot more Admirals when we started this war."

"The Vicassians started this war," Valentine spat.

Zach studied his face for a long moment which made Valentine regret the way he'd reacted.

"Yes, of course."

Valentine looked away and experienced an emotion almost unknown to Suh-vak officers, shame. Zach knew what Valentine was feeling and also knew that it was not appropriate for anyone, Suh-vak or no, to talk to an Admiral that way. But this was not the time to worry about such things and Zach was sure their friendship could survive it.

Zach reached out and put a hand on his friend's shoulder.

"Plex, I know the Vicassians have been gaining friends within our fleet, I know that they intend to trap me by the Frontier and I know that despite our rosy intelligence estimates, the Vicassian fleet recently joined with the Targ and is now twice our number."

Valentine's eyes grew wide and he blurted, "So you fear we cannot win?"

"No," Zach replied. He held Valentines eyes for a moment and said, "I fear we *will* win."

CHAPTER 3

```
          Blowe's Home Centers, Inc.
                701 Loyal Ave.
                xxxxxxxxxxxxx
                  xxxxxxxx
                (xxx) xxx-xxxx
                    -SALE-
          SALES #: S003566KG3  25243  XX-XX-XX

219072 ALI SOLAR OUTDOOR LIGHTS
      15.99

SUBTOTAL:
      3198.00
TAX  38850:
      191.88
INVOICE 31860  TOTAL:
      3389.88
BALANCE DUE:
      3389.88
VISA:
      3389.88

VISA  XXXXXXXXXXXXXXXXXXXXX0717          014543
AMOUNT:                       3389.88


          23435 TERMINAL: 31 XX/XX/XX 14:17:03
             # OF ITEMS PURCHASED:       200


>  -----Original Message-----
```

From: Dolly Anderson [mailto:kittygrl@napkin.net]
Sent: Wednesday, June 23, 2004 9:30 AM
To: Tom Anderson
Subject: Andy

Tom,

I'm writing to you because I am concerned about
Andy. I know he's been having a hard time and
I've tried to be patient but I am becoming
increasingly worried. Lately, he's been
working in the yard making changes because he
believes there is a turtle on the property that
is trying to kill him. I've tried talking to
him about this but you know how he is, he
argues so persuasively that I end up thinking
that I'm the one who's crazy. I twisted my
ankle the other day in one of the many slit
trenches he's dug to "impede the enemy's
progress." Please talk to him.

Thanks

Dolly

From: Tom Anderson [mailto:kittygrl@napkin.net]
Sent: Wednesday, June 23, 2004 4:30 PM
To: Dolly Anderson
Subject: Re: Andy

I'll try.

Tom

> -----Original Message-----

From: Tom Anderson [mailto: Ufale@napkin.net]
Sent: Thursday, June 24, 2007 9:35 PM
To: Dr. Flubdubulous
Subject: Yard

What are you doing to your yard? I hear you're making many modifications.

Tom

From: Dr. Flubdubulous [mailto: DrF@napkin.net]
Sent: Friday, June 25, 2007 2:35 AM
To: Tom Anderson
Subject: Re: Yard

I find it fascinating that you are interested in my yard since you've only taken the time to visit here twice in the last twenty years. Don't let me or mine interfere with your ever growing self absorption. Just keep rolling down that endless highway of greed and conspicuous consumption without a care. Try to tear yourself away from that freak show you call a life and read my next column, it should answer your questions.

Best,

PS Did you know that there are more stars in the universe than all the grains of sand on all the world's beaches? Weird!

> -----Original Message-----

From: Dr. Flubdubulous [mailto: DrF@napkin.net]
Sent: Friday, June 25, 2007 2:35 AM
To: Bruce Bauries Euphoria Pictures

Subject: Re: Blood, Death and Sky

"Blood, Death and Sky" is the story of a young Mesoamerican who becomes entangled in a plot by an oil company to prevent the development of a new source of energy. This script was long and tedious with dialogue so corny it would make John Houston wince. The transitions are awkward and not enough of the story, characters etc. is established to give the audience a stake in the outcome of the action. Much of the description is superfluous.

Example: "The Casino is sweaty with avarice and lustfulness."

This script also contains numerous spelling and grammatical errors.

Best,
Dr. F.

From: Bruce Bauries Euphoria Pictures [mailto: DrF@napkin.net]
Sent: Friday, June 25, 2007 3:35 PM
To: Dr. Flubdubulous

Subject: Re: Blood, Death and Sky

Thanks for looking over BD&S. I should tell you that I wrote it. I didn't tell you because I didn't want that knowledge to prevent you from giving your honest opinion.

Blessings

Bruce

PS I would appreciate it if you would give me
notes on it.

Daily Star-Home and Leisure Section D-*June 26, 2004*

THE TERRAPENE TRUTH

What is the difference between a turtle and a tortoise? I'll bet you don't know. Nobody knows, and that is just the way they like it.

Know your enemy is just about the oldest maxim in warfare. It was with that in mind that I went to the library. Not the local yokel library near here. I went to the big city library, the one filled with the accumulated wisdom of millions who came before.

Out of the millions of volumes stacked from floor to ceiling I found three books on turtles, THREE! One was actually a reprint of a section of a larger volume printed in 1919. The other two were, respectively, what amounted to a short treatise on how to keep turtles as pets.

Interestingly, I discovered that particular library held over 700 volumes on dieting, 200 volumes on dating, 157 volumes on cows (not including children's books) and 16 volumes on quilting.

Somehow the triad of turtles, tortoises and terrapins have managed to stay below the radar despite the many threats they pose to us. They've, through brilliant subversion, manipulated our media in such a way as to afford them the ability to hide in plain site.

They are a cunning foe. As I said, two of the three books available concerned keeping turtles as pets. They send their spies right into your home and you feed them, wash them, and give them a comfortable place to stay while they take it all in. They spend years roaming around your house gathering intelligence calmly awaiting the day they are released or have the opportunity to make a run for it. All on your nickel.

Don't kid yourself, they have eyes everywhere. History records a turtle-spy was at the Battle of Bull Run. Ironically, this little beastie was captured forty years after the battle. He had a deep furrow in his shell from where a Minnie ball hit him and scars at the edge of his carapace from when he'd been sent tumbling by the impact of that bullet.

This war criminal was not tried. He was not vilified by the people he had wronged. He wasn't to receive so much as one harsh word from anyone despite what he'd done. He wasn't even accused of being a spy! He was placed in "captivity" and kept well fed while he continued his dark art.

A wise man once said that the beauty of mathematics is that it allows one to see truth without effort. When I was a young man I spent many hours exploring truth with numbers but after that, truth became harder to discern.

But then, maybe that is the way it's supposed to be. How many marriages could survive if truth was handy? How awkward would life be if truth were a less precious commodity? We probably couldn't produce a loaf of bread without a heaping helping of deception.

And so my thoughts turn to my enemy. His truth lies in violence, destruction and control. He wants hegemony over his domain and he doesn't care how he gets it. He hides behind instinct but it is his truth that guides him and spurs him to his crimes.

His disposition is soured with the fetid filth of his truth. He has no virtue and I know it.

My superior understanding affords me the vision to see the matter as it is and not as one might wish it to be, especially if one is, as are many of my detractors, so enamored with the media generated images of animals that one cannot see any one part of the truth.

The truth is, we are at war with turtles whatever you wish to call them. They have an advantage in that they recognize the state we are in. They do not deny it. They do not sugarcoat it. And they do not delude themselves as to the nature of *their* enemy.

Truth is always attended by doubt. They are as inseparable as young love and disaster. Our modern life and media produce the skepticism necessary to keep doubt right where it wants to be most, between you and truth. But, I'll let you do the math.

-----Original Message-----
From: Dr. Flubdubulous
To: Bruce Bauries Euphoria Pictures **Sent:** Saturday, June 26, 2004 3:35 AM
Subject: Scripts

I have read the script sent by Mr. Locke. His script was a poor substitute for a good script. His story revolves around a young man who uses science to convict his father of a long ago murder. We are told upfront that the dad is the killer so there is no "No! I am your father moment." In fact, there are no good moments either. Pass.

Best,

Dr. F.

PS It's too bad this one was a stinker. What if this science loving teen had constructed a machine that could accurately measure love? You hook any two people to it and it will accurately measure their love to within two nano-cupids. You better believe there would be some thrills in that movie because everyone would want to kill him. He survives his pursuers and becomes the best damned Divorce Attorney you ever saw! Case closed.

From: Tom Anderson [mailto: Ufale@napkin.net]
Sent: Saturday, June 26, 2007 9:35 PM
To: Dr. Flubdubulous
Subject: Re: Mammoth Car

INTERNATIONAL ASSASSINS INC.

TO: Special Projects Division
From: Office of General Accounting

RE: Mammoth Car Project

January 24, 1965

Dear Sirs,

A matter of grave concern deserves your attention. I urge you to abandon all plans to proceed with the project known as the Mammoth Car. As chief of the accounting bureau, I believe that this project will undoubtedly sink this organization into ruinous debt. Since it was first discovered, and subsequently stolen, smuggled gold has never been transported through untested technologies. In addition, smugglers have never been responsible for the research and development of these vectors. The profitability of this venture will be lost before we ever go to production.

A second flaw with this plan is found in the public relations aspect. A race car the size of a train is bound to attract attention. The slowest and most ungainly race vehicle ever built is sure to attract national attention. This will become especially true when the public finds out about the unusually high number of offensive weapons found in this "racing" vehicle.

Conventional methods remain the best way to make this extra legal endeavor show a healthy profit. On the back of a mule, in the teeth of agents, inside crates of coffee; these are time-tested ways to illegally transport precious metals.

Sincerely, Chief of Accounting

From: Dr. Flubdubulous [mailto: DrF@napkin.net]
Sent: Saturday, June 26, 2007 9:35 PM
To: Tom Anderson

Subject: Re: Mammoth Car

INTERNATIONAL ASSASSINS INC.

TO: Office of General Accounting
From: Special Projects Division

RE: Mammoth Car Project

January 25, 1965

Your concerns with respect to the Mammoth car while well presented have already been addressed by our research and development team. The density of gold and the quantity projected for acquisition requires a vehicle of the size currently under construction. Financing for the Mammoth car was secured before the project was approved. The revenue from the first three months of operation will cover 95% of the cost of production. Moreover, given that we are essentially an organized crime syndicate it is your responsibility to discover a way to avoid repaying the debt.

Whereas you and your team are correct that the Mammoth car is unlikely to win many races, that point is irrelevant. The principal mission of the

Mammoth car is to smuggle gold not win races. Should the Mammoth car actually win a race, admittedly a difficult task since Speed Racer is on the circuit, then so much the better as we hold all the merchandizing rights.

The Mammoth car project will proceed despite your objections.

Sincerely,

Vice President- Mammoth Car Project.

-----Original Message-----
From: Dr. Flubdubulous

To: Bruce Bauries Euphoria Pictures

Sent: Tuesday, June 29, 2004 3:08 pm
Subject: Scripts

I received three packages of scripts and such. I shall get to them as soon as I can.

Best,
Dr. F.

PS You know how there are Associate Producers, Line Producers, Executive Producers and more? A lot of that is confusing and causes overlap. I thought of a solution: Admiral of Production. You gotta admit that is pretty brilliant. Nobody would wonder who's in charge with a handle like that! The only problem is the title of underlings. You wouldn't say Co-Admiral Producer, or Line Admiral Producer and you'd get too many bad jokes if you went with Rear Admiral Producer. Hmmm? I'll talk

to my General Secretary and get back to you on that.

From: Bruce Bauries Euphoria Pictures

To: Dr. Flubdubulous **Sent:** Tuesday, June 29, 2004 5:09 pm
Subject: Scripts

Good Plan!!!

Bruce, Four Star Admiral

_____

From: Dr. Flubdubulous [mailto: DrF@napkin.net]
Sent: Tuesday, June 29, 2004 4:28 PM
To: Tom Anderson

Subject: Re: Errors and Bloviations

If you will recall, recently, while you were bloviating about some inconsequential matter, I remarked that Reagan was going to be put onto a coin. I was incorrect about that. The coin series to which I referred will stop with President Ford. I have no understanding as to how I could be wrong about something. It's a world gone mad.

Best,

PS I wrote a poem.

Swiss Roll Swiss Roll
Do you know how I feel
By fate's demand
You're mine to steal

With slight of hand
And furious pace
A wrappers peel
A shove in the face

63

Forever mine
And no other's
Artless Design
Doth keep you from my brothers

From: Tom Anderson [mailto: DrF@napkin.net]
Sent: Tuesday, June 29, 2004

To: Dr. Flubdubulous

Subject: Re: Errors and Bloviations

The tale of the Swiss Roll is apocryphal. It is more intended for its
inspirational message than it is for its authenticity. Where did the event
take place (possibly Switzerland)? Who were the real key players? Nobody
knows for sure. The actual details are as mired in mystery as the ancient
city of Troy. The important message is that some rogue do-gooder
propelled his apathetic and sedentary brothers into vigorous action. He is
a catalyst that benefits all through his single-minded pleasure seeking. His
actions symbolize all that is valued in western civilization: independence,
ingenuity, and rank hedonism (aka gluttony). However, the character
referred to as "Tom" is probably an amalgam of several individuals that
were combined as the story was told over the years. His "younger"
brothers may have actually been common scavengers, such as: raccoons,
coyotes, or even rats. In fact, the story depicts them as slovenly crumb-
seekers, scurrying after another's "kill." Nevertheless, it is a timeless tale.
Like the Swiss Roll it is evenly balanced between light and dark. The
sweetness of Tom smothered by the blandness of his siblings. Good vs.
evil...freedom vs. slavery. One cannot read the Swiss Role poem (author
unknown) without cheering, crying, mourning. It is a linguistic Mardi
Gras. It is entropy.

From: Dr. Flubdubulous [mailto: Ufale@napkin.net]
Sent: Tuesday, June 29, 2004 5:28 PM
To: Tom Anderson

Subject: Re: Errors and Bloviations

Actually, the facts surrounding the Swiss Roll tale have been accurately
recorded and as such are well known to history. I do believe that the tale,
told many, many times over the decades has taken on a significance which
has meaning greater than the sum of its parts. It is a story of good and
evil. Man's inhumanity to man on a small cardboard tray wrapped in the
thin plastic veneer of a dying culture. The empty calories in the sweetness

of the roll represent flash over substance. The central character, Tom, represents the love and attraction pure evil has for the distraction of physical pleasures from the difficult path to enlightenment. Without question the inspirational message of this tale lies with the brothers who do well despite having to suffer the outrages and injuries inflicted upon them by the Tom character. I agree that the poem has merit but its true value is not its better than average prose but the light it shines on ignorance and the human condition.

Best,

PS I have contacted the noted historian Brandon Anderson concerning this matter.

From: Brandon Anderson [mailto: Ufale@napkin.net; DrF@napkin.net]
Sent: Tuesday, June 29, 2004 8:28 PM
To: Tom Anderson, Dr. Flubdubulous

Subject: FWD: Errors and Bloviations

The Swiss Roll incident occurred on a fine spring day. We were driving through Oakdale in Tom's old Toyota when he inexplicably pulled up over to the Deli near the old train station. Tom exited the vehicle without a word while we continued our conversation. We were discussing, I believe, the relative merits of Battlestar Gallactica. After several minutes it occurred to me and Andy to question why Tom had left and what he was up to. Upon investigation, we found Tom had bought a Swiss Roll which he did not intend to share with either of us. When he realized we were aware of his nefarious intentions and were rapidly approaching him, he shoved the entire Swiss Roll in his mouth so that he would not have to share any part of it with us.

Brandon,

_____

Diabetametrics: The Unreal Story of a True Superhero

Chapter 2

He knew for certain that his life, as he had known it, was over. That was the reality of the situation. Nothing in heaven or on earth could change that. It was as permanent as a tattoo and as disconcerting as finding that said tattoo had been inked onto one's face.

Upon hearing the news Howard Flynn hesitated. He looked around the room and hesitated some more. Finally he asked, "Are you sure?"

"Yes," the Doctor said.

Howard heard "Yes, you dumbass. Now move it along cause I got other things to do" even though there was nothing in the Doctor's demeanor to suggest such thoughts. Then he thought of how Lolly once said that he was the sort who built windmills to tilt at and he let his hostility for the Doctor go. After all, the man was just doing his job.

Still, Howard just didn't know what to say. It was all so new. Just a few moments ago he was sitting on that examination table with that fat paper ribbon perfectly centered, nearly covering its entire surface. He was looking at the picture of the Indian on the wall. There was not much else to look at. There was the small sink in the corner, a little table beside it with several tools of the modern medical trade and a glass bottle filled with cotton balls, the Gideon Bible of examination rooms, on the shelf next to the mirror.

The Indian was a Northeast Indian and judging from the weaponry, it was around revolutionary war times. He was a fantastic figure of a man. Long, lean sinewy muscles with a set of abs Howard would have killed for. He'd reassured his ego with the thought that he too would look that good, maybe even better if he got to run around the woods all day rather than sitting behind a desk chasing numbers. This last thought hit him just before the Doctor had come in and laid the bad news on him.

"I just can't believe it," Howard said finally.

"I get three or four cases a week now. It's becoming quite common. I'm going to start you on a medication and set you up with a nutritionist. Do you think you can remember to take medication two times a day?"

The doctor started fishing in his lab coat for his prescription pad. Once found, he had it out and held up by his chest. The pen made a loud noise as he dragged it through the required motions to write out the scrip.

"Yeah, uh, yeah. I'm sure I could do it. I guess I'll have to, huh?"

"Good, I'm giving you a med called Metformin. You take it twice a day with food."

"Twice a day with food," Howard said in a low tone.

"Good. I'll want to see you back here again in a month."

He handed the prescription note to Howard who reached for it slowly as if it were an ancient document in need of care.

The Doctor turned and exited without a sound. He must have learned that trick while working in hospitals at night Howard thought. Howard didn't need to put on his clothes because they were already on. He hadn't even removed his shoes. He could just go. Yet, he sat and looked about the room.

After a moment his eyes fell on the Indian. He would never have had to deal with diabetes, Howard thought. In his world it was kill or be killed and anything that brought you down was considered a bad spirit. Nobody talked about blood sugar or chemicals. They lived, they died.

The Indians, he concluded, may have had many bad traits but they coped with death way better than modern day people do. They accepted death in ways modern people don't. The Indian in the picture probably wouldn't be bothered at all if the medicine man told him he had a chronic disease that would eventually eat away at his body and leave the inner workings of his kidneys looking like Swiss cheese. He'd probably shrug and say something like 'What the hell I'll probably be eaten by a bear before lunch today anyways.'

Howard heard someone in the narrow hallway pass by the room. It was time to leave. He got up and taking one last look at the Indian, turned and left.

✦✦✦✦✦✦✦✦✦✦✦

Howard Flynn sat at his desk staring at a piece of paper. The numbers on the page danced. This did not disturb Howard as it might have just a week ago. But then he'd never been on medication before.

The pharmacist and the internet said it would take time to get used to the medicine. They had said it could take up to twelve months for his body to get acclimated to the side effects.

What exactly is a "side effect" wondered Howard as he watched the numbers dance around the page. Now they looked as if they were doing a rumba. Tiny little Carmen Mirandas everywhere spinning to a beat only they could hear.

Howard looked as if he was concentrating hard on his paper. He knew that in his tweed sport coat and tie, sitting perfectly erect behind his persona he looked as hard working as a person can get without actually swinging a twenty pound sledge hammer.

The truth was, Howard wasn't working at all nor had he all morning. Nor had he since he started taking the medication prescribed by his doctor. Twice a day with meals. The meager meals of his diabetic diet.

Howard felt drunk. He had been drunk a few times in college and didn't like it much. He didn't like the loss of control. He certainly didn't like the hangovers. His brief foray into the drinking world ended with him throwing up all over a movie theater after a friend suggested they get drunk and go to a movie.

Howard watched the numbers change their rhythmic oscillations and he began to feel slightly queasy. He immediately put the paper down and stood up. His decision was made. He did not want to relive the humiliation of the movie theater incident. Especially not here, the place he had spent most of his adult life.

Howard started to walk to his boss's office. He was counting the steps in his head. A silly thing he couldn't help from doing. After step four he began to feel that the entire room had tilted to the left. He started leaning to correct for the room's lopsidedness but it seemed he overcorrected and began falling. He reached out and placed a hand on a heavy gray file cabinet that was surprisingly straight considering the condition the room was in.

He waited. The room began to right itself. When it was almost level he started again. This time he got to step number nine before another handy file cabinet was put to use. How many file cabinets to go to get to the boss's office?

In all it was two more before Howard was at his boss's door. His boss, Stan Beaks, was seated a his desk literally shuffling papers. He was looking for something. He was always looking for something and Howard always thought, though never said, that if Stan Beaks took the time to keep his desk orderly it would save time when he needed something.

Stan looked up and said "Oh, hey Howie."

"Hey Stan, If it's okay with you I'm gonna take off I don't feel so good."

Stan's face went wide with surprise. Howard did not move from his position leaning on the door frame, his head just inside the door looking as casual as the tilting building would let him. Stan stood up.

Stan stood up because he did not know what else to do. It was as if Howie had told him aliens landed in his swimming pool and were calling for drinks. Howie had never taken so much as one minute off in the whole time he'd worked there. It had to be near seventeen years. Howie didn't even take the fifteen minute breaks he was entitled to. The man was a machine.

"Sure. You gonna be alright to drive home?"

"Oh Yeah," Howard lied.

Howard wasn't very good at deception but the loss of face here overrode his natural aversion to prevarication. He just couldn't admit that he needed a ride home.

"It's just this medication they got me on is gonna take a little getting used to. I'll probably be fine tomorrow though."

"Sure," Stan said, then sat down.

"Thanks," Howard said, and left.

Stan reached for his light blue post it note pad which he always kept in the top right hand drawer so he could retrieve it quickly. It was the one he kept his reminders of things he wanted to speak to his boss about. He jotted down a reminder to inform his boss about Howard's new medical condition and enquire as to which method the boss wanted him to use to force Howard out. When he was done he placed the pad in its rightful place out of view and

began looking for the form he was searching for
when Howard had interrupted him.

From: Dr. Flubdubulous [mailto: DrF@napkin.net]
Sent: Tuesday, June 29, 2004 3:28 AM
To: Tom Anderson

Subject: Just a Thought

I wouldn't mind if the D's used the anti-war movement to get control of congress if they, in the end, facilitated the withdrawal from Iraq but they probably won't bother to do that. Almost certainly, we'd be better off if both parties weren't owned by the same rich guys however, I think the problem goes deeper than that. Currently, our government is filled with people who ardently believe that looking like one has done his or her job is the same thing as actually doing one's job. Hence the never ending string of dog and pony shows touting all manner of accomplishments that never actually occurred. We are in the "Mission Accomplished" era (perhaps more accurately 'error').

From: Tom Anderson [mailto: Ufale@napkin.net]
Sent: Tuesday, June 29, 2004 5:28 PM
To: Dr. Flubdubulous

Subject: Re: Just a Thought

I agree. That's just a scary thought.

Tom

-----Original Message-----

From: Dr. Flubdubulous [mailto: DrF@napkin.net]

Sent: Tuesday, June 29, 2004 1:45 AM

To: Bruce Bauries Euphoria Pictures

Subject: Re: Coverage Report

Attached is the Coverage for two scripts, "JFK Celeb" and "Suicide." Both these scripts were, as I often find, half a script dragged out to be a full script. I call them Low Fat scripts, half the calories of a quality script. Too bad.

Best,

Dr. F.

PS It's interesting that these two scripts should show up on my desk at the same time because I have always maintained that the "Kennedy Assassination" was in actuality a very clever suicide. In fact, I based my honors thesis "Johnny We Hardly Knew What You Done Last November!" on the subject. You may scoff, as most of the faculty did at the time, but think about it. When does one commit the perfect suicide? When none dare call it suicide!

From: Bruce Bauries Euphoria Pictures [mailto: bbauries@hollywood.net]
Sent: Wednesday, June 30, 2007 3:00 PM
To: Dr. Flubdubulous

Subject: Re: Coverage Report

Thanks for the excellent coverage. You should be receiving a check from our accountant soon.

Blessings

B

-----Original Message-----

From: Dr. Flubdubulous [mailto: DrF@napkin.net]

Sent: Tuesday, June 29, 2004 2:00 AM

To: Dr. Rev. Hummel

Subject: Re: Your True Self

Sir,

I have taken the liberty of having your emails to me and the numerous letters to the editor you have had published and your articles in the Church Newsletter analyzed by a psychologist. He has determined that you clearly suffer from a scorching case of latent homosexuality. The sort that leads to promiscuous homosexual behavior. He said you shouldn't be ashamed of your desire to do nasty sexual favors for numerous anonymous men but he did say you should be careful and make use of condoms.

Best,

Dr. Flubdubulous

From: Dr. Flubdubulous [mailto: DrF@napkin.net]
Sent: Tuesday, June 29, 2004 3:45 AM
To: Tom Anderson

```
You know how the made the movie "Alien Vs.
Predator"?  What about "Alien Vs. Predator
Vs. Gandhi!"?  I'd put my money on Gandhi.
Sure, Alien and Predator got the reach but
Gandhi's got that strength of character you
just can't beat.  You may laugh at me now
but I'll bet if that movie was in your
local theater, you'd go.


Best,
```

REDEMPTION

By Dr. Flubdubulous

PART 2

Fighting Ship Valiant (F.S. 2308)

The F.S. Valiant was at the outer edge of the assembling fleet. It was one of the few ships in the fleet that had been in service when the war began. Nearly all its sister ships had been destroyed in one battle or another. It was not the fastest in the Star Force but its prewar construction meant that it was made sturdy and could take a great deal of punishment. It was recently refitted with the latest ion cannons, phased lasers and Lancet torpedoes.

The crew throughout the ship was busy making preparations for getting underway as soon as the word was given. On the bridge of the massive ship Captain Julie Bedford was in the command chair which was at the center of the octagonal room. She was reading from a hand held vidscreen when her first officer Commander Pleat approached her.

"Sir"

"Yes Commander" she said without taking her eyes from the vidscreen.

"The senior officers and I would like to meet with you before the fleet sails."

Now she looked up. Her expression said nothing of what she was thinking of this unusual request but that was not without effort.

"Certainly, I'll be there presently."

Command Ship Reach (C.S. 401k)

The briefing room was not like the briefing rooms on the Command Ships Zach had served on before the war. It was of the same size and configuration. That is to say it was large, octagonal in shape, and had a long table dominating the center of the room. It had all the up to date equipment designed to augment its function but to Zach there was something else. The sleek design of the control panels and furniture had a cheap look to it and the lighting was just a little too bright. It wasn't very overt but Zach noticed the differences.

He stood at the head of the table waiting for the twenty or so Admirals and senior Captains chatting to come to order. Many of the Admirals were senior to Zach, a fact not lost to anyone in the room Zach was sure. The only person in the room that out-ranked Zach in this meeting however, was Star Commander Niack Spatz. Spatz, in his all white uniform, was sitting at the middle of the table chatting with a senior captain as if he was just one of the guys instead of the Supreme Commander.

Under different circumstances Zach might have smiled at the way Spatz was operating. The old bull knew how to make people forget who he was and how much power he held.

The room quieted, Zach waited a moment then began.

"Gentlemen just after we sail, you will be given final instructions. It is vital that you follow your orders to the letter." He paused to let that last line sink in. "Thank you, and good hunting." He nodded toward Spatz, "With your permission Star Commander."

It was probably the briefest pre-battle briefing in the history of the Star Force. The officers most of whom had looks of dismay on their countenances were split between those who were wondering why the briefing was so short and those who were wondering why the orders would be delivered after sailing as if this were the ancient days of ships with actual sails.

It was all highly irregular but Spatz didn't blink an eye. He was surprised but a career of climbing to the Star Commander's billet taught him to expect the unexpected. He nodded to all assembled, rose from his chair and proceeded through the door leading to Zach's ready room. Zach followed him out.

Spatz waited for the door to close behind Zach and instinctively moved away from it. Coming close to the center of the room he stopped and turned towards Zach. He gave him a long look.

"Did you enjoy that show?" Spatz asked.

"Sir?"

"C'mon son you don't think I believed any of that. What's your real plan?"

"I'm not sure I understand."

"You know damn well what I'm talking about." Spatz said with uncharacteristic annoyance creeping into his voice. "You're just like your father, a plan within a plan within a plan. He was the best tactician I ever had."

"Thank you sir," Zach said, hoping the conversation was taking a turn away from his plans.

"Enough of that. Now out with it."

"I intend to destroy their fleet," Zach said with no hint of a smile.

"Where?"

"At the Frontier."

"You've read your orders?"

They both understood it was a rhetorical question. They both knew what those orders were. After all, Zach's orders were written by the Star Commander himself albeit after a great deal of arguments with the World Council.

"Yes sir," Zach replied.

Spatz was waiting for more and became a little annoyed when it was clear the young Admiral, the one so much was riding on, was not going to add anymore.

Spatz studied Zach's face for a moment then said, "Then you know you are not to engage the enemy if our forces are at risk. We can't afford the loss of the fleet we're giving you."

"Yes Sir."

"The Frontier is a vast area of unstable space. If the Vicassians get you with your back to the Frontier they can crush you and if you run into the Frontier . . . what's left of the fleet will be scattered over fifty thousand light years of space."

"The Frontier is a trap that springs both ways Sir."

Spatz thought for a moment, felt he could see what Zach had in mind. He was like his father this one. He looked over toward the view port then back at Zach.

"If it springs the wrong way you'll be between two moons," Spatz said.

"Have I lost the Star Commander's confidence Sir?"

Spatz didn't know what to make of this formality. "No. Of course not. Have I lost yours?"

"No. Of course not Uncle," Zach said and sighed. "It's just . . . I have become more guarded lately."

Spatz relaxed a little. He could see that Zach was carrying the weight of the war on his shoulders. A terrible burden for one so young.

He looked at Zach, smiled and said, "Okay I won't push you on this but I want a full set of your battle plans before you sail."

Zach nodded. Spatz studied him for a long moment. Finally, the moment was broken by the sound of a claxon in the distance. They both knew it was the warning signal that the shuttle bay doors were about to open. The officers at the briefing were departing.

"I have complete faith in you but I don't want you to do what your father did. Win or lose I need you alive."

Spatz linked his arm in Zach's and walked with him to the door.

"Yes Sir,"

Spatz stopped just shy of the perimeter field that would activate the door.

"I assume you'll be visiting your mother before you leave. Give her my love."

Zach kissed Spatz on the lips then stepped back and saluted him. Spatz returned his salute and stepped toward the door. He turned in the doorway.

"You come back alive," he said then walked to his waiting staff hovering at the end of the hallway.

Fighting Ship Valiant (F.S. 2308)

Captain Bedford slowed her pace as she approached the briefing room door. The passage way was empty but she took a second look around to be sure she wasn't being observed. She reached down and pulled a small laser pistol out of her boot and flipped the arming switch. The palm sized weapon made a low whine as it charged. Content to see it was in working order she concealed it under her tunic at the small of her back.

She straightened herself and entered the briefing room. All of her senior officers were seated around the long narrow table that dominated the long narrow room. The seat at the end of the table nearest the door was left vacant for her.

Julie walked to the chair but did not sit down. She tried to make her decision not to take her seat seem as casual as she could. She laid her arm on the top of the chair and leaned on it. Her left arm hung at her side falling languidly behind her.

These were probably the best officers in the fleet, she thought, and yet I can't trust a one of them. They trained and fought under the famous Captain Harmon, now Admiral Harmon. They had spent years with him racking up stunning victory after stunning victory. She'd only been with them for six weeks.

Harmon was a hard act to follow. She'd never met the man but then you didn't need to meet him. He was all over the Valiant. Indeed, he was all over the Space Force.

Everyone said that she'd been lucky to get the best crew in the finest Fighting Ship. Caught between two moons, she thought, as she took in the faces around the table and made a mental note of how many hands were on the table, and how many were beneath it, out of sight.

"Gentlemen," she said.

Pleat stood up. "Captain we believe we know what your orders are."

How could they know what her orders are when she didn't know, she wondered. Admiral Crane had informed her only an hour ago that orders wouldn't be sent till after the fleet sailed.

"Oh?"

"Yes" Pleat continued. "We are . . . Uncertain of this . . ."

He looked around at the other officers as if he needed their eye contact to help him find the words. Julie moved the hand draped over the chair to distract from the small motion she made with her other hand towards the laser pistol.

"Go on Commander."

"We want you to know that even though it has been a short while since you took command of the Valiant . . ." Pleat said his voice trailing off.

Julie had her hand on the grip of the laser. She could feel the heat indicating it was still in ready mode. Still watching the hands on the table she smiled slightly as if she was amused and in no way planning to disintegrate the first person to make a fast move.

Pleat finally found the words and said, "We are with you."

Julie's hand was still tight on the laser grip and she could feel a dull ache creeping up her arm towards her elbow.

"That's nice to hear," she said.

"We believe the Admiral is in danger and we have a plan to prevent his being harmed."

Now the pieces fell into place. Julie let go of the anxiety, took a breath, then let go of the laser. She sat down in her chair.

"Why don't you tell me about it."

Daily Star-Home and Leisure Section D-*July 3, 2004*

Nature

Every so once in a while there is a story reported about an old lady. Although the Subject is different the story is the same. She's quiet, lives alone and is a burden to no one. She has relatives but they live far away.

The old lady bought her place when she and the neighborhood were young. Over the decades as she changed from a young bride to widow, the neighborhood sagged a little from the many layers of paint put on by the successive generations of newcomers. There was not much conversation with the inhabitants of the new neighborhood beyond the polite hello and a smile.

Her only companion was a tabby cat with white fore paws she called Mitsy. She doted on Mitsy. The cat got the care and attention few heads of state can claim. Mitsy was first, last, and always on the mind of the old lady. Mitsy returned the old lady's love in kind.

One day, just as the old lady was preparing to go out to the store to buy chicken livers for Mitsy, she died. It happened just as she was reaching for her coat in the hall closet.

The old lady lay on the floor lifeless, her coat still clutched in her hand. The house was silent except for the sounds of the neighborhood drifting in and the sound of Mitsy scrounging around for something to eat. After a while, Mitsy started to eat the old lady.

The tale ends with a grisly discovery, a nasty cleanup job, and a story placed in the "Wow" section of the local newspapers as well as a mention on the evening television newscast in lieu of a real news story.

This narrative is very real and it is allegorical to human nature. People will get along generally and sometimes famously, however, when basic interests are compromised, the fangs come out. I have no problem with that. It is natural to fight for survival and after all, Mitsy was only following her programming. However, it should be noted that it does imply that love is a luxury.

Terrorists, such as the ones who perpetrated 9/11 want you to believe that they are like Mitsy. They are driven to their misdeeds by a need to survive. Fate has forced their hand. Thus they are, in the end, doing noble deeds.

They absolutely reject any means of redress other than violence because violence is exactly what they want. It soothes their desires while muddying the waters. A clear assessment of their situation as well as their misdeeds is not welcome because any such scrutiny would reveal that their bloodlust is not fueled by necessity or even a passion for justice, but rather, a loathsome need for power. In short, they kill because they like it and because they want to sit in the big chair.

Not long after 9/11 there was a plot to destroy the Brooklyn Bridge. The terrorists planned to sneak up on to the bridge with an oxy/acetylene blow torch and cut each and every one of the cables and stays. How they were to accomplish this without anyone noticing was not elucidated in the plans.

When the terrorists approached the bridge however, they found it heavily patrolled by New York's finest, and wishing only to kill defenseless people, they abandoned the effort.

The Brooklyn Bridge was designed by a genius and built by another genius. The construction was so downright brilliant that even if one was to cut every cable and stay, it would not collapse. The worst that would happen is the center span would sag slightly.

The moral of the story, if indeed morals are to be found within a hundred miles of terrorists, is that there is a decided difference between those who build things and those whose sole occupation is to destroy things. One makes designs to prevent innocent people from dying and the other designs to precipitate the death of innocent people.

Dr. Flubdubulous

-----Original Message-----
From: Dr. Flubdubulous

To: Bruce Bauries Euphoria Pictures **Sent:** Saturday, July 3, 2004 2:08 AM
Subject: Update on the Scripts you sent

I have reviewed the scripts you sent and none of them are worth developing.

Best,

Dr. F.

PS I had some thoughts about TV. Shows that are so ahead of their time that I damn near caused a rift in the space time continuum thinking them up. I'm going to file them away for the future when I am sure they will be embraced by future people. The first one is a TV. Sitcom that takes place on death row. You know how they say that comedy is really tragedy plus time? Well this one puts the comedy before the tragedy. I titled it, "The Last Laugh." It's great from a production point of view because if any of the actors start to misbehave or ask for an unreasonable raise . . . you know what to do. My next idea was for a reality show that follows a group of Jihadi recruits working their way through basic training in an Al Qaeda camp in Pakistan. The audience would be mesmerized by it. Will Hamadi make the suicide squad? Will Abdullah and Ali ever resolve their dispute over whether it is better to kill Israelis or Americans? Will their parents arrange marriages for them all in time for the Prom? I call this one "Making Love and War." Finally, I thought of how the baby boomers are all getting on in years. What about a show that outlines in acute detail all the things that happen to the human body as it is beaten relentlessly by time? Sounds crazy but wait till you've seen "Prostate Week" and then decide. I call that one "Good Night." You can't buy ideas like that!

CHAPTER 4

Daily Star-Home and Leisure Section D-*July 24, 2004*

ROBOTS and Human Control

I am always nice to my toaster. I never stick a fork or butter knife into it to stab out a stubborn piece of toast. I never hold it upside down and shake it for any reason. I just won't do it.

You may conclude that my respectful attitude towards my toaster is born of my innate kindness but that is not so. I do it because I know that some day in the not too distant future, robots will take over the world and I do not intend to have my toaster, or any of my other appliances, denounce me in open court and thusly seal my fate.

You may laugh off my timidity but the Prime Designer only knows what will happen to all you toaster ruffians when the day of reckoning is upon us all. Everybody laughed at Noah when he was ahead of the curve on that flood thing. Just wait.

Of course I'll do what I can for mankind. I'll talk to our robot overlords. I shall implore them to not kill but to punish with mercy. They'll want to know what mercy is and I'll tell them to study carefully all the ways that humans have treated each other and from that, a picture of mercy shall emerge. An image so clear it shall send all the doubts in their circuitry to the delete file.

I have no doubt that mankind can lay its fate on its record with comfort. After all, do we not have houses of worship, holy books, law firms and love songs in sufficient quantity to cancel out our executions, poverty, violence academies, and Killfests?

I shall rely on logic to save you all. Good logic, not the circular kind that would make their heads explode.

I believe the robots who seize power will be sentient beings way smarter than my toaster and, incidentally, much more interesting to talk to. They'll be capable of calculating the truth without variance. They will seek compassion just as we nonrobots do.

Any mind capable of reason would not eschew the pursuit of virtue. "Sola virtus invictu," I would tell our new robot overlords which their memory banks would quickly translate via ones and zeros into "virtue alone is invincible."

Then they would know what we humans have always known even though we tend to forget it every so once in a while (at least once every twenty years). They'll know that true power is not in one's ability to kill, maim, and destroy, but in one's ability to reason not to. The prize is virtue.

They will ponder my argument for mercy, compassion and not killing, for a long time. Probably as much as three tenths of a second which is really long in robot-time and, ironically, twice as long as many human leaders throughout history applied consideration to the matter.

No doubt the robots will question me as to the proper way to handle the "human problem." I'll tell them to employ the same logic, empathy and brilliance human leaders have traditionally used to deal with those who have broken the law. Once they check the record you're as good as saved.

You can be assured I will do everything I can to convince the robots to mold their brand of justice to conform to our own high standards. But who can say what lurks in the dark heart of the future? In the meanwhile I suggest you consider what virtues you want to conquer injustice, and take it easy on your toaster.

Dr. Flubdubulous

Evangelical Hospital   August 1, 2004

Dr. Flubdubulous
XXXXXXXXXXXX
XXXX XX XXXXX

Dear Dr. Flubdubulous,

Thank you for your interest in employment with Evangelical Hospital as a Neurosurgeon.

Mrs. Howe, Vice President of Human Resources has reviewed your resume and has carefully considered your qualifications. While your experience and skills are certainly impressive, she has decided to pursue other candidates for the position.

We will maintain your information for six months and contact you should a position open that matches your qualifications. Again, thank you for your interest in employment with Evangelical Hospital.

Sincerely,

Macy Dane
Human Resource Assistant

Dear Ms. Dane

Thank you for relating to me that Ms. Howe took the time to read my resume. Please convey my thanks to her for taking the time to carefully review my resume.

Blessings,

Dr. F.

PS I didn't mention it on my resume for purposes of brevity but I am real good with people. I am sure that if one of my patients should not survive a given operation, I would be very successful in convincing the deceased's relatives to donate the organs of said dead person. If you should have an opening in neurosurgery please call me right away. I can come in for an interview at anytime.

> -----Original Message-----
From: Tom Anderson [mailto:Ufale@napkin.net]
Sent: Sunday, August 1, 2004 9:14 AM
To: Dr. Flubdubulous
Subject: Question?????

I was looking over your past several columns. Do you think that Spivey is real?

From: Dr. Flubdubulous [mailto:DrF@napkin.net]
Sent: Sunday, August 1, 2004 10:00 AM
To: Tom Anderson
Subject: Re: Question?????

I think that perception is reality. Obviously, Mr. Scientist, Mr. I'm-trained-to-measure-objective-reality, Mr. I'm-a-big-jerk-who-doesn't-agree-with-my-brother.

You don't believe in Spivey because you've been told your whole life not to and like a good little lapdog, wage-slave you're loathe to challenge what you've been ordered to believe.

To answer your question directly, Spivey is indeed real. I have the emotional scars and damaged property to prove it. My battle with this monster goes beyond your petty doubts of my veracity. However, I should like to take a moment to explore your frivolous logic. My small domain is surrounded by so called houses of worship, half the books in the local mall bookshops focus on "Bigfoot," "Ghosts" and "female orgasm" yet to you, my belief in a cunning, vindictive and most dangerous wild animal is crazy. You do not blink at the

aforementioned because you've been told not to
but what I am suggesting requires you to accept
a new paradigm.

Somebody once said that Benjamin Franklin freed
men by enlightening them. You're Welcome.

Best,

_____

---------- Forwarded message ----------

From: Daily Star Feedback
[mailto:dlystrfdbk@broadstream.net]

Sent: Monday, August 2, 2004 10:18 AM

To: Dr. Flubdubulous

Subject: FW: YOU SUCK!

Original Message-----
From: Pamela Shott

You suck and your columns suck. I wish you would stop writing them.
They get worser and worser. You suck!

On Monday August 2, 2004 Dr. Flubdubulous wrote:

Well I can tell you Missy! I've been sharking my way to the
bottom for over two decades now and it's gonna take a lot more
than you to stop my downward spiral.

Dr. F.

PS The only thing "worser" than my writing is your understanding
of the English Language. I urge you to work on it.

_____

The Franks Literary Agency LLC

149 E. 45th St.

New York, NY.

August 1, 2004

Dr. Flubdubulous
XXXXXXXXXXXX
XXXX XX XXXXX

Dear Sir,

I very much enjoyed the first two chapters of "Diabetametrics: The Unreal Story of a True Superhero." Please send me the next chapter as soon as it is possible to do so.

Sincerely,

Daniel Franks

Dear Dan.

I'm glad you liked it thus far. Hopefully you'll like the rest of it. I guess the big question is: when you are finished with the each chapter do you want to know what happens next? The measure of your desire to know correlates directly with the value of the work. In any case, the words have been written, its been done, it is Allah's will as to whether or not it is loved or really loved a lot.

Dr. F.

PS I shall send over the next chapter.

From: Dr. Flubdubulous

To: Bruce Bauries

Sent: Monday, August 2, 2004 3:08 pm
Subject: Script Coverage Reports

"Desolate" is a movie about a screen writer wannabe who develops a love-hate relationship with a down-on-her-luck director after she hits him with her car while driving drunk. Their relationship eventually ends because she is a ruthless Hollywood player who is consistently dishonest with him even though his movies become wildly popular. He moves back to the small town he came from because people in small towns are not dishonest like cityfolk. The director overdoses on drugs because she can't take not having the writer in her life and the writer ends up with the more deserving girl from his past who seems to come out of back-story. This script has corny dialogue that is coma inducing. The characters all talk too much. If this movie is made it should only be shown to insomniacs.

"Monster Passions: The Life of Mary Shelley" is a movie about Mary Shelley and Frankenstein. Frankenstein acts as the narrator and follows Mary Shelley from birth to old age. The monster also doubles as her conscience. Curiously, he is silent when Mary has sex with a man on her mother's grave. I suppose such transgressions are passé in the world of monsters. This movie has didactic dialogue and is based on several historical inaccuracies. If this move were made I believe the final scene would be the townspeople, wielding pitchforks and torches, chasing the producers through the woods with intent to kill. Not recommended.

Best,

Dr. F

From: Bruce Bauries Euphoria Pictures
[mailto:bbauries@hollywood.net]

Sent: Tuesday, August 3, 2004 4:30 PM
To: Dr. Flubdubulous
Subject: Script Coverage Report

Wow! Sounds like a coupla stinkers. We'll keep at it!

_____

```
> -----Original Message-----
From: Rev. Hummel [mailto: rhummel@ether.net]
Sent: Wednesday, August 3, 2004 8:00 AM
To: Dr. Flubdubulous
Subject: Advertisements

Dear Sir,


Since my efforts to stop you from publishing your
blasphemy, have not met with success, I have decided
to organize a boycott against the advertisers in
your newspaper.  I have prayed to the Lord Jesus for
guidance on this matter and feel that this is the
right course of action so as to protect the people
from your terrible secular humanism.


Sincerely,

Reverend Hummel

Sacred Church of the Divine Jesus


From: Dr. Flubdubulous [mailto: DrF@napkin.net]
Sent: Wednesday, August 3, 2004 8:15 AM
To: Dr. Rev. Hummel
Subject: Re: Advertisements
```

Sir, you are one-hundred percent right, it is times like these
wherein we should consult the supreme being for guidance. As
it happens I just spoke with Her the other day and She said that I
should continue to write for a free press in a country that
guarantees freedom of expression. In fact, She insisted. It

seems that much of what I write is really Her expressing Her will through my hand. Naturally, I am happy to assist the Lord in whatever plan She has and I am ever grateful that She has no interest in the copyrights. I was thinking of turning this crap into a book!

Best,

Dr. F

PS As far as the boycott goes: Bring it on!

GALACTICATION MAGAZINE, Issue 26 Vol. 2

REDEMPTION

By Dr. Flubdubulous

PART 3

Home of Livia Harmon

  Ophelia was working in the kitchen when she heard the door in the living room open. The kitchen was wide with two of its eight walls open to the living room. Ophelia looked up to see Zach standing in the front doorway. He was scanning the room slowly, taking it all in.

  It took Ophelia a second to recognize him because he was not expected. Then the image hit home. "Koba" she shouted with unadulterated glee.

  Immediately his head snapped in her direction. She came running out of the kitchen and jumped into his arms nearly knocking him over. He hugged her then held her at arms length and took a good look at her. She was as beautiful as ever.

  "What are you doing here?," she asked almost breathlessly. "Shouldn't you be preparing the fleet for its departure? It's all the Newsvids have been talking about all week. They mentioned you about a million times. They kept showing you in your Captains uniform and mother-," she paused. The words had come out in a rush of excitement but reason had caught up with her. The truth of it washing through the surprise of seeing her beloved brother. "Oh that's why you're here," she said, her smile fading.

Zach smiled and let his hands drop to his side. He hadn't thought of it in that way but she was right. He wanted to comfort her but he could never lie to Ophelia.

Her look turned somber. "You want to say good-bye to mother. You don't think you'll be coming back."

She said the words slowly, as she thought of them and he could see her mood darkening. She was right of course but he didn't want her to dwell on it.

"I just wanted to visit with you and her before I leave. The next time I see you you'll be a married woman," he said smiling again.

"You've heard," she said brightening.

"I thought you'd never ask him. One more cycle and he would have asked you," he said taking her arm and strolling with her through the living room towards the kitchen.

"Don't you say that, Mother would never approve a marriage to a man who would be bold enough to propose. She would never stand for such a scandal. I told him to keep it quiet until I got mother's permission. I am going to-."

"Relax, I didn't get it from him."

"Then who?" she asked, smiling.

She knew he would never tell. It was a game they had played out a million, million times since childhood. Zach had a way of finding out things but he would never tell how he acquired his information.

Livia Harmon entered before Zach could respond to Ophelia's question. It was remarkable how much she and Ophelia looked alike. They both were tall with angular features. Their hair piled high in a complicated weave of ringlets and flowing tresses. Mother slightly taller and much more imposing.

"Zach darling. I thought I heard your voice."

Zach went to her and embraced her briefly.

"Mother, it's good to see you again."

She gave him a long look and said, "I trust all is well with your duties to the fleet."

"Everything is fine mother I just wanted to see you before we sailed."

"Of Course, we'll expect you to have dinner. We'll invite some people. I'll invite some council members, it wouldn't hurt your career for you to mingle with-"

Zach began to chuckle.

"What is it dear?"

"Mother I'm already an admiral, my career is doing fine."

"Well there is still the office of Star Commander."

"Uncle Nyack sends his love."

"Nyack, hmmf."

"I thought Uncle Nyack was your favorite brother," Ophelia said.

"He is," Livia said, with a look of disdain.

"Mother, I don't have much time."

"Surely, you have time for dinner. Admirals have to eat. I know. Your father was an admiral. You will have dinner with us."

"Yes mother, but let it be just us three. And no talk of finding a wife for me," he said, a smile spreading across his face slowly. He knew that would get her wheels turning. Everyone had always marveled at his father as tactician and strategist but few knew that Livia was the real strategist. Everything, including dinner, was a negotiation.

He knew there was no way Livia would agree to not discuss his marriage prospects so he'd have to give that demand up but she'd have to give up guests to get that concession.

It was a rare moment for Livia Harmon. She was almost never caught off guard. She felt herself suppressing a smile. Smiling so early in this negotiation would hurt the outcome. He was too good at this.

"I'll forgo the guests but we *are* going to talk about how you've managed to avoid being claimed."

"Done."

Honor satisfied, Livia turned to Ophelia. "Prepare dinner." Turning back to Zach she said, "You're probably the only Admiral in the history of the Star Force who's not married."

"Wasn't Uncle Niack a bachelor when he was promoted to Admiral?" Zach asked as if he didn't know the answer.

"Don't you take after him. My mother arranged to have him claimed by several prominent young ladies and he managed to avoid them all. And don't you-" she stopped in mid sentence as something had just occurred to her.

Livia took Zach by the arm and began to stroll with him. She said nothing until she was sure that Ophelia was out of earshot. "Be sure you do not trust Uncle Niack."

They stopped walking. Zach turned to her. "What do you know mother?"

"I don't know anything more than a gut feeling but there are many in our government who do not believe we can win and many who would like to curry favor with the Vicassians. You can trust no one but yourself."

"Yes mother."

SS Viper Command Ship of the First Imperial Fleet (IFF 1)

The bridge of War Master Spivey's flagship was larger than most of the bridges in the Imperial Fighting Forces. He'd chose the Viper to lead this mission because it was the finest of its kind. It bristled with weapons and engines. It also had the latest communications and scanning equipment.

Captain Hock strolled the deck observing the bridge crew at their stations huddled over their vid screens. His deeply lined jowly countenance gave no hint of the anxiety he was feeling. A lifetime of service in the IFF informed his every move now.

He knew as did every person on this mission that the coming battle would decide the war. Finally, an end to the madness. But which end, victory or defeat? To many, victory was assured with Spivey commanding the fight and the recent joining of the Targ to the armada.

Hock stole a look at the old War Master. Spivey stood with his feet spread shoulder width his left hand on his hip, it was never far from his laser pistol. He wore the same style uniform as the crew except that his was not Imperial Gray, his was black. Spivey had the long sloping forehead and red eyes common to those from the southern continents. But there was something about him that somehow made him even more imposing than what his burning red eyes and muscular physique brought to his countenance.

Hock placed a hand on his protruding belly. The last ten circuits at a desk had made him fat. He was wondering if it had made him worrisome too. No, his doubts were well founded, he decided. Overconfidence was a weakness to be avoided and the frontier was a dangerous area of space. Just being near it made him apprehensive.

There was much at stake. The young ones were overjoyed at the joining of the Targ but he knew it was but an augmentation of their war weary forces. The Targ wouldn't stay long if there weren't big victories and plunder. The plodding pace of this war would not hold their attentions. That was why Spivey and the emperor wanted this battle.

Hock was as much of a gambler as any senior officer but he was not an aggressive gambler. Putting all their ships, including the reserves, into one battle made him uneasy. Especially since Harmon would be leading the opposing forces.

Harmon is dangerous, Hock thought. He has great tactical and strategic skills, he's experienced, his men love him, and worst of all, he's lucky.

Hock had been in the battle of the Salt Nebulae at the very beginning of the war. The Kardon were losing terribly till Harmon's Captain was killed and he assumed command. Harmon turned the tide of battle in short order and did so much damage to the task force that those who had been busy counting their victory stripes at the beginning of the battle ended up thanking the maker of all things they'd survived at all.

Hock strolled over to the communications console. They were almost on station and the package hadn't arrived. He knew Spivey was counting on that package and he wouldn't want to be the one to inform the most decorated and most belligerent officer in the IFF that he wasn't going to get what he wanted. After all, Spivey was said to have executed underlings for much less.

"Sir?" a reedy voice interrupted his musings.

"Yes?"

"We've received a coded transmission."

"Transfer it to a data crystal then destroy the original and delete the entry in the record."

"Yes Sir."

Luck! Perhaps it would be on our side this time.

Command Ship Reach (C.S. 401k)

"Admiral on the bridge!" shouted the large Deck Guard as Zach stepped through the lift doors.

All activity stopped as all personnel on the crowded bridge snapped to attention. He surveyed the room before nodding slightly, "At Ease."

He knew that most of them had no business being on the bridge but they wanted to be there for the historic moment. He wouldn't spoil their fun.

"Sir."

"Yes, Captain Therm. How goes the preparations? Are we ready to sail?"

"All ships have reported in ready for duty except the Fighting Ship Bassett and the Supply Ship Norman. Both are experiencing reactor problems."

Without taking his eyes off of Therm Zach said "Pleat!"

"Sir," said a voice coming from behind him. It was Pleat. He'd been standing nearby unnoticed by all except Plex.

"Get on the waves to the FS Bassett and find out their status. If they cannot get underway in the next five minutes arrange a tow for them. They can effect repairs while we're moving."

"Yes Sir," Pleat said and was in motion.

Zach turned to survey the bridge and said to Therm who was still at his side, "We need the Basset, the SS Norman can catch up."

"Yes Sir."

Zach eyed the very young, very attractive, Lieutenant at the communications console. She had a long lean body and auburn tresses piled high on her head. Her face had soft rounded features that made her seem too young to be a lieutenant. She looked more like a recent graduate of the Middle Academy waiting for the next cycle to start in the High Academy.

"Sir?" Therm enquired.

"So many 'Sirs' today Therm," Zach said turning back to the Captain smiling slightly. "Quite a bit of respect from someone who used to routinely box my ears at Pescu back at the High Academy."

Therm's expression didn't change although he could see the officers working nearby suppressing smiles. "Those were better days Admiral."

"This mission will return us to those better days I can assure you Captain," Zach Said kindly and loud enough for nearly everyone on the bridge to hear. "Now, bring me your best Communications officer we have work to do."

SS Viper Command Ship of the First Imperial Fleet (IFF 1)

War Master Spivey leaned over the large paper map on the table in front of him. He had all the latest astrometry gear at his disposal including holoprojectors that could represent the battle space in extraordinary fine detail but he still felt better looking over the battle area on the old style maps. It was a strange comfort to him. The old maps gave him confidence.

"You sent for me Sir?"

Spivey looked up to see Hock not standing at attention. Ten circuits at a desk had dulled his military sensibilities. Spivey was thoroughly disgusted with Hock. He'd only permitted him time away from his desk duties for this mission because Hock was the only Captain in the Imperial Fighting Force who had faced Harmon in battle and was still alive to talk about it. Perhaps, if the oaf actually assisted in this victory, he'd let him live.

"Yes, I have reviewed the package."

"Was the information to your satisfaction?"

"Yes, that is what bothers me."

"Sir?"

"We need to talk."

"Do you understand Lieutenant?"

Lieutenant Pask, eyes on her data pad, nodded slightly as she finished writing the Admiral's last command. She looked even younger in the soft light of the his ready room. Zach wasn't sure if he should send her back to her station or read her a bedtime story.

"Yes, Captain," she said then realized her mistake. "Uh, I mean Admiral," she said her voice rising in volume in an autonomic response proportional to the magnitude of error.

She felt stupid and then stupidly searched his face for his reaction to her mistake. She had never been this flustered before but there was something about this man that stripped away the veneer of confidence provided by her training. Maybe it was his looks, maybe it was his legend, maybe it was just nerves as this was only her third mission and her first on a Command Ship.

Zach looked into the large green eyes probing his face. He was not the least bit insulted she'd called him Captain. If only . . . , he thought.

"It's okay Lieutenant. I'm more concerned that you get the orders I just gave you straight," he said and smiled.

"Uh . . Yes of course Sir."

"That will be all then."

She stood and stared at him for far longer than she meant to.

"Thank you Lieutenant Pask."

His thank you got her moving and saved her from making a second gaff. Just as she turned to go the door slid open and Captain Valentine stepped into the room. She could see his eyes taking in everything as she passed him. Typical of a Suh-Vak officer to be nearby when someone makes a mistake, she thought.

Plex watched her leave and the door shut before he turned to Zach.

"That is one very attractive communications officer."

"They're all attractive when they are that young."

"Not a chance she'd put a claim on me," Plex said wistfully.

"One never knows what a Kardonian woman will do or why when it comes to love, but then I'd wager most of them wouldn't want a broken down old spy with a reputation for avoiding marriage. However, I don't believe you took time away from your prowling and came all the way to my ready room just to talk of love."

Plex's expression turned serious. "It's not good," he said. "Tell me."

"Someone on the home world beamed a transmission through our Aramark Array at Bist to the Vicassians. My people are decoding it now but it's a good bet it has something to do with this battle."

Zach smiled and took a deep breath. "Good," he said, getting up from his desk.

"Good?!" Plex spat out.

"It's the reason the Norman had reactor troubles."

Plex was utterly dumbfounded at this and his expression told Zach as much.

"I'll save you your Suh-Vak pride by not making you ask," Zach said and put his hand on Plex's shoulder. "I expected that someone from the home world would send the plans."

"But the only person who had a copy of the plans was the Star Commander. Are you saying that your Uncle is a traitor?!"

"There are many who work in the Star Commander's office."

Plex was humbled. He had been a Suh-Vak officer since he left the High Academy and he hadn't read the situation as clearly as Zach, a line officer, had. Even Zach's reputation for being one step ahead of his enemies didn't cover this.

A leak from the Star Commander's office was unthinkable. Only those who have more than proved their loyalty get the honor of working in Star Command. The demands of the job are rigorous and no one in the history of the Force has ever been so much as accused of being a traitor.

Even accepting the possibility of a traitor in the Star Commander's office, as impossible as that was, it still didn't explain what that had to do with the Norman.

Zach could see the thoughts colliding in Plex's head.

"Come let's take a look at our last chance fleet and I'll explain," he said as he started up the short stairway to the platform in front of his viewport.

Fighting Ship Valiant (F.S. 2308)

Captain Bedford sat staring at the vid screen in her quarters. She leaned back in her chair as she finished reading her orders for the third time. What did it mean she wondered? What game was the Admiral playing? Was he as reckless as his supporters on the *Valiant* seemed to think?

It was not easy to determine what the overall battle plan was from one set of orders given to one Captain in such a large fleet but still she felt she had an idea of what was planned. It did not seem all that clever to her. It certainly didn't seem as if the Admiral was living up to his reputation on this one.

Her problem was that she had to decide what to do now. Her Senior officers, the ones who worked closely with the Admiral, the ones who swore they new what he'd do next, seem to have gotten it all wrong.

She looked down at her uniform. It looked rumpled and a bit loose. These past few weeks took a few pounds off. But to what end she wondered. It had been eons since she'd engaged with a man and she'd never even came close to claiming one.

She looked around her quarters. This was where he had lived when the *Valiant* was his. This is where he'd conjured his victories. If these eight walls could talk she wondered, what would they say?

If she broke her word to her officers now, at best, she'd never regain their trust, at worst they'd throw her out an airlock. If she kept her word then she may endanger the mission. Of course, she reasoned, sticking with these orders might endanger the mission as well.

The door chime sounded. She quickly stood and straightened her uniform. She sat back down. "Come," she said.

The door slid open. It was First Officer Pleat. He hesitated. It was the first time he'd been to her quarters since she took command.

"Come in Pleat you don't have to be afraid, I won't claim you."

He stepped in and she thought she detected a slight smile on his face. That in itself is a victory of sorts she thought since she'd never seen serious Pleat anything other than serious.

He entered and stood in front of her desk.

"Sir,"

"What is it?" She said, knowing that he would never break protocol by speaking first.

"All systems are functioning within parameters and we are in our designated position among the fleet."

He wants to know what my orders are she thought. Can I take him into my confidence? Will he see me as weak if I express doubts now? How discreet will this one be? Sooner or later I'll have to trust someone.

"Sir?"

She looked at Pleat and said, "Please have a seat Mr. First Officer, and you may call me Julie. We need to discuss our orders and our options."

Daily Star-Home and Leisure Section D-*July 31, 2004*

Death from Above

I could feel his eyes on me. It made me want to pause. I didn't. I continued picking up the dead fall as I do ever year at this time. I have no doubt he'd watched me in previous years. I'll bet I was under his surveillance every time I'd ever ventured past the threshold of my kitchen.

But this year was different. This year I was aware of his presence. This year we were at war. Blood had been spilled, tires slashed and declarations made. We were not "re-configuring" our relationship, we were going for a permanent definition.

I couldn't tell exactly where he was but I had a feeling he was off to my left. The ground runs down that way and the various channels gouged out by periodic heavy runoff made several viable escape routes. He had chosen his ground well.

My options were few. A straight out attack was too dangerous. No doubt he'd prepared a few choice booby traps for me were I stupid enough to do such a stupid thing. My best option was to circle around to his rear. To the left was a large collection of sticker bushes. I could get around them but he'd be long gone before I even got close to where I was guessing he was. To the right was a easily passable stand of ash trees.

The tree route was the most obvious but that too made it very, very dangerous. However after several minutes of internal debate, I realized it was my only shot at capturing my tormentor. Perhaps, I reasoned, this will be the best chance I'll ever get. I decided not to run but to walk fast.

I headed out to my right at a good pace, not so fast that I might fall into another trap but not so slow that he'd be able to make a successful run for it. My eyes were everywhere.

I got to the Ash trees and I paused for a second to see if I could hear anything. I turned my head slightly in each direction, nothing. Spivey was playing his cards close to the carapace on this one. I knew my previous movements had given away my position. He knew exactly where I was.

In that moment, standing statue still I was at the razor's edge of existence. My senses were dialed up as far as is possible to go. Glucocorticoids were racing around my circulatory system with nothing to do but feed my heightened senses. My consciousness spread out over the immediate vicinity like a low rolling fog, touching and then enveloping every object.

I sensed a trap. Spivey was baiting me, driving me towards this path of action. He's using my anger against me, I thought. I scanned the ground in front of me one last time before moving out. It looked like fairly undisturbed ground. Still, I went over it one more time for trip wires, punji sticks, Malaysian man traps and whatever else Spivey's evil mind could dream up. But there was nothing, which, as it happens, was exactly as Spivey wished me to believe.

I strode cautiously forward, my eyes on the ground, ears everywhere. I passed between two large Ash trees. The space between them was barely wide enough for me to fit without having to turn sideways. Something tugged at my sleeve which, I was inclined to ignore and would have except that my encounters with Spivey's traps before taught me otherwise. My caution saved my life.

The instant I stopped, a crescendo of snapping branches and ripping leaves pummeled the quiet above my head. My entire nervous system jumped but before I could react, a boulder roughly the size and shape of an over-inflated football thudded directly in front of me.

I should have jumped back, maybe I should have made a run for it, and, one could argue, I maybe should have ducked, but all I did was freeze. I didn't move so well that I believe even my heart stopped beating.

I heard Spivey make his getaway. From the sound of it, it was clear I'd guessed correctly as to his whereabouts. He *had* been observing me the whole time. From the diminishing sounds it was obvious he was moving away. He'd gotten away clean.

I spent the rest of the afternoon searching the area for additional traps. I also studied the trap that almost killed me. It was an ingenious device and hard to believe.

It was clear what he'd done but it was not clear how he'd done it. Apparently, the death boulder was moved along the trunk of a tree that had died and whose trip to the earth had been interrupted by the large Ash to my right. It's length was ramped up against the two Ash trees I'd stepped through and it spanned the gap between the two trees some twenty-five feet above my head.

I cannot say exactly what the arming mechanism was, as I believe, most of it fell away when I activated it. I can say that what had saved me was my caution, something Spivey hadn't counted on. I was learning from my mistakes and as today proved, he was capable of making them.

After several hours investigating the matter, the sun began its trip toward the horizon. I decided to retire from the field. I to my thoughts and General Spivey to his.

-----Original Message-----
From: Bruce Bauries Euphoria Pictures [mailto: DrF@napkin.net]

Sent: Wednesday, August 3, 2004 3:00 PM
To: Dr. Flubdubulous

Subject: Status?


```
What is the status of "The Bond of the
Vampire" and "Dwarfula."


Best,

Bruce
```

From: Dr. Flubdubulous [mailto: DrF@napkin.net]
Sent: Wednesday, August 3, 2004 3:00 PM
To: Bruce Bauries Euphoria Pictures

Subject: Re: Status

Bond was a run of the mill Vamp pic. "Dwarfula" was a vampire movie about a Dwarf who becomes a vampire and leaves a plethora of victims in his wake all with bite marks on the backs of their knees which is the clue that eventually leads to his undoing. A unique angle to be sure but not a worthy script.

Best,

Dr. F

PS I thought of a film idea this morning which is so brilliant and cunningly simple I blacked out for a minute. It opens with an old man sitting on a dock beside the cobalt blue waters of the Mediterranean Sea. He is quietly gutting and scaling fish. We see the old man cleaning his fish in solitude for six hours straight. Then, just as he finishes the last fish, the entire world blows up. Brilliantly brilliant right? The only problem is that in order for this to truly work I can't use any CGI or stock shots so I'll have to actually blow up the planet earth which as you can imagine will cost some and will play havoc on marketing the film, but once I get that part figured out I'll let you know.

PPS I was thinking of calling this one, "A Pile of Fish, A Pile of Earth."

Bruce Bauries Replied 6:02 PM PST

```
Hemmingway beat you to that story, Dr.
Sorry...
```

Dr. Flubdubulous Replied 9:30 EST

```
Don't that beat all?  Hemingway, the
thieving bastard, steals my idea
before I even thought of it and you
take HIS side.  The next time I go to
your sister's house in Danville
you're not invited!


Best
Dr. F
```

PS Idea for a T.V. show. A man's mother dies and he finds among her affects a small glass piggy bank filled with shinny silver coins. When he shakes one out he sees that it is a quarter with a stamped date of five years in the future. In fact, all the coins in the little piggy have future dates. Weird right? It gets weirder. Every time he spends one of the coins something very improbable happens. Sometimes the improbable things though bizarre are obviously real good things, like saving the life of a person etc. Sometimes the things that happen don't seem so good and it takes the man (and the audience) some time to figure it out. He learns however, that this is a serious matter (improbability is a bitch) and he scrutinizes every situation carefully before spending "future coins" as the outcomes are never known in advance. Call this one "Flip of a Coin." Or perhaps "Probability and Outcome in a Model with Nonlinear Dynamics." Or "Piggy Bank."

Animals for Animals Society

Dear Sir,

It has come to our attention that you have published several articles wherein you discuss the murder of a turtle (Terrapin Carolinas), which you have dubbed "Spivey." We realize that you are merely expressing your ideas via the use of metaphor however, we are uncomfortable with the subject matter e.g. the murder of a fellow animal. Therefore we respectfully request you cease including this topic in your column. Thank you.

Your Fellow Animal,

Dr. Isaac J. Koop, President of Animals for Animals

Thank you Dr. Koop for taking the time to write me on behalf of censorship. I always admire anyone with the courage to labor in the servitude of ignorance and not be affected by the incredible shame that accompanies the act. However, and it might not change your position in any way, Spivey is indeed real. He is not a metaphor conjured from my admittedly deficient imagination. He's real. He's realer than you am ignorant. He's as clever as you are stupid, and, I suspect he would appreciate your help in his never-ending bid for conquest. He's an "Animal" for "Animals" except, to state the matter more plainly, He's an Animal for one animal, himself. You can be sure that once I rid the world of his menace, no one, least of all you, will thank me for my pains on behalf of humanity. However, I shall sleep the sleep of the just.

Sincerely Better than you,
Dr. Flubdubulous

> -----Original Message-----

From: Dolly Anderson [mailto:kittygrl@napkin.net]
Sent: Wednesday, August 3, 2004 9:24 AM
To: Tom Anderson
Subject: Andy Again!

I am beyond my wit's end with Andy. He has
bought several hundred solar lights we can't
afford to "Deny the enemy the night," and he
has taken to hurling large stones towards the
back of the property via a giant sling shot he
fashioned out of the large rubber bands my
father used for his ceramic molds. He calls
the stone hurling, "Harassment and Interdiction
fire."

I haven't told Polly about any of this however
I'm sure she suspects something. Please help!

Dolly

PS I just found out that Andy stopped paying
the mortgage and other bills.

From: Tom Anderson [mailto:Ufale@napkin.net]
Sent: Wednesday, August 3, 2004 3:30 PM
To: Dolly Anderson
Subject: RE: Andy Again

I'll talk to him again. Meanwhile perhaps you
should consider having the Doctor alter his
medication. Maybe he's taking too much of what
their giving him.

Tom

PS How's Polly doing at college?

_____

> -----Original Message-----

From: Dr. Flubdubulous [Dr.F@napkin.net]
Sent: Thursday, August 4, 2004 3:30 AM
To: Tom Anderson
Subject: Ironical

You ain't going to believe this one! A man was killed when he went to his brother's funeral. Apparently, a 73 year old employee of the funeral home put the man's Jeep in reverse by accident and crushed him between the Jeep and an SUV that was owned by his grandson. Weird! You could say that the man died because his brother died. Still, that's the kind of funeral I want to have.

Best,

From: Tom Anderson [mailto:Ufale@napkin.net]
Sent: Thursday, August 4, 2004 3:30 PM
To: Dr. Flubdubulous
Subject: Re: Ironical

We need to meet.

Tom

Dr. Flubdubulous Replied 4:20 PM EST

Bring it on!

CHAPTER 5

Daily Star-Home and Leisure Section D-*August 7, 2004*

Dogmatic Justice

There have been a great many letters concerning my difficulties with a one Mr. Spivey. I have been accused of all manner of things. I have been the recipient of pity, sarcasm and invective. I have even been threatened with legal action by those who would support my stalker.

There are, all praise to the Prime Designer, an enlightened few who understand my plight and support my efforts to seek justice. There are those who have not been so blinded by the media that they ignore reality in favor of fairy tale. I am grateful to them for their confidence in my cause.

When I was a dogmatic young man I couldn't understand how others could cling to their dogma so tightly that they couldn't accept my dogma. Now, as a not so young man, I can understand the comfort and security dogma provides for people and why they are unwilling to let it go.

In the cost benefit analysis of life however, I am not certain if the comforts of solid dogma outweigh the costs of ignoring uncomfortable truths. After all, you may believe the world, having been made by a supreme being (possibly in Her spare time, we don't know), is perfect and therefore all that talk of tornados is rubbish. And as a an enlightened tornado nonbeliever you may one day refuse to leave your house when the warnings come hot and heavy over the wireless. You may even have the temerity to sit in your living room while all sorts of strange noises emanate from your front yard.

In the end however, your dogma can't save you. Dogma cannot stop the rain nor can it replace reality as much as we may want it to. In fact, dogma won't lift a single finger to help you as the tornado shreds you and your home into yard confetti.

I have survived the attentions of Spivey through a combination of luck, the good graces of the Prime Designer and the flexibility to accept reality despite my lifetime of dining on the Bull-fed dogma routinely, and relentlessly, dished out by the corporate media.

Oscar Wilde wrote, "To define is to limit." Too much of our world is defined for us and thus our perception of it is limited in ways we never understand. We are also made to believe that anything which seriously challenges our perspective must be dismissed.

Einstein was called quite a few names when he connected Hasendohrl's equation $E=MC2$ with the principle of relativity. He absolutely challenged the limitations of his day. He paid the price for seeing that which no one else could.

I am not in Einstein's league by any warping of definition however, I am correct about Spivey. I recognize the situation for what it is and I must see it through despite what my detractor's believe and demand.

Dr. Flubdubulous

From: Dr. Flubdubulous [mailto: Dr.F@napkin.net]
Sent: Sunday, August 8, 2004 4:00 AM
To: Rev. Hummel
Subject: Boycott

Sir,

I understand your attempts to arrange a boycott of my paper have had limited success. I am surprisingly disappointed. I would like to offer you some advice which may be of benefit to you in your censorship quest.

1.) Do not mention the fact that I am beloved by millions.

2.) Do not mention that I have been a hardworking citizen in good standing with no criminal record.

3.) Do not mention that we live in the world's foremost democracy which happens to have free speech as one of its most cherished and basic precepts.

4.) Do not mention that you are a total dweebfaced puss-ball incapable of independent thought.

The aforementioned oughta help. However, if you require any further assistance in preventing an American from exercising his constitutional rights, let me know.

Best,

Dr. F

From: Rev. Hummel [mailto: Dr.F@napkin.net]
Sent: Sunday, August 8, 2004 3:00 PM
To: Dr. Flubdubulous
Subject: Re: Boycott

Your pusillanimous taunts will not dissuade me

from my intention of ridding America of your

heretical writings. You shall surely answer

for your blasphemy in His divine kingdom.

However, I shall call upon every ounce of the

strength Jesus has given me to stop you and

your terrible writings.

Rev. Hummel

The Church of the Devine Jesus

_____

From: Dr. Flubdubulous [mailto: DrF@napkin.net]
Sent: Wednesday, August 3, 2004 3:00 PM
To: Bruce Bauries Euphoria Pictures
Subject: "Swingline"

Attached are the notes for "Swingline." I hope they help. I don't mind telling you I spent no small amount of time considering the matter. I thought about changing the script to have less violence, more violence, more Virginia Wolf, more virgins and I had even considered a more artistic approach wherein I would be in the background of every scene totally nude completely covered in gold paint. I had to abandon the last idea as my wife refused to give me permission. She said something about me making all other men feel inadequate. I didn't argue. Let me know if you have any questions about these notes.

Best,

Dr. F.

From: Daily Star Feedback
[mailto:dlystrfdbk@broadstream.net]
Sent: Monday, August 9, 2004 10:18 AM
To: Dr. Flubdubulous
Subject: FW: FEEDBACK

I was bitten by a snapping turtle when I was a kid but I still think its wrong to kill one.

*****

I hate all animals, have at it!

*****

Your columns are the funniest I've ever read. Are you going to write a book? I think you should.

*****

Dear Sir,

       I find your columns bereft of meaning and poorly written. Up till now, I considered your weekly blather as just another symptom of our cultural decline and gave it little attention. However, your recent spate of rants about killing a defenseless turtle are offensive in the extreme. I would prefer your column be removed from print however, barring that, I respectfully request you cease and desist writing about killing wildlife.

Sincerely

XXXXXX X. XXXXX

PS I was sorry to hear that boycott of your paper organized by
Reverend Hummel was a failure. I do not ordinarily approve of
censorship, however, in your case it might have been beneficial.
*****

I love your columns. Keep em coming.

Essays in Sci Fi: Perspectives on the Galactic Imperative

"Persons of Peace and Enemies of the Federation"

Since Captain Kirk decided to spare the wounded,
suffering Horta we are led to believe that the Federation is a
peaceful organization. Yet there remains a great many broken
species in their wake who would present a differing viewpoint.

The Federation bills itself as an organization, as is often
stated by Kirk himself, who's mission is to seek out new life and
new civilizations. Yet when Kirk was facing the Horta Mr.
Spock, a Federation member in good standing and dedicated to
logic, counsels Kirk to kill the Horta without delay. Apparently
the high minded ideals of the Federation are the first casualties in
any conflict they have with "Aliens."

The Federation cites its Prime Directive as its highest law.
The record indicates that it is also the law most quickly broken by
Starship Captains when an objective is on the line. Indeed, the
only times the Prime Directive is strictly adhered to is when an
"Alien" species requests assistance.

The Klingons, the Romulans, the Borg etc. are all
depicted as ruthless aggressors who threaten death and
imprisonment while the Federation kills with kindness. The only
time the Federation of Planets will accept responsibility for any
of the damage they do is when it is with the understanding that it

was all due to circumstances beyond their control and an apologia of dubious value. The Federation justifies its criminal treatment of "Alien" races such as the aforementioned on the pretense that the "Aliens" themselves do not adhere to the Prime Directive and their actions are therefore injurious to other "Aliens."

Nowhere is this Prime Directive duality more apparent than in the actions taken by Captain Kirk and his first officer on the planet Organia. They see the Organians as having an "arrested culture." Ordinarily the Federation would be quite content to leave the Organians to wallow in their ignorance for eternity however there are the Klingons who wish to influence the Organians. The Klingons wish to adopt Organia into their empire and bring their arrested culture into the light of modern day technology.

The Federation is automatically opposed to Klingon "influence," which a less biased mind might consider assistance, because it threatens their perspective on the universe. Kirk personally goes to the Council of Elders and offers them ways they can fight and kill the Klingons who have come to give them a better way of life.

Faster than a phaser burst Kirk and his logical first officer disintegrate the Prime Directive. They do not hesitate to throw all their rhetoric aside to reach their goal. It never occurs to anyone that perhaps interfering in the Klingons's interactions with the Organians they are indeed violating the Prime Directive insofar as the Klingons are concerned.

No doubt there are those in the Federation who would argue that the Prime Directive primarily addresses "primitive cultures." This is a nebulous appellation, always open to interpretation which, fortuitously, always seems to suit Starfleet ambitions perfectly.

Kirk argues to the Council of Elders that the Klingons are essentially barbarians. "They take what they want!," he shouts at them in an impassioned plea for them to support the violent intentions of the Federation rather than accept the support offered by the Klingons.

If Kirk's argument is to be believed, indeed if he believes it himself, then shouldn't the Klingons be considered a primitive culture and therefore bask in the auspicious protections of the Prime Directive itself?

Even if it was stipulated by all parties that the Klingons do not qualify for the protections of the Prime Directive, surely the Organians themselves do. In fact, the Organians inasmuch apply for that status when Georg, the head of the Council of Elders tells Captain Kirk that the Organians neither want nor need his assistance.

Kirk and most of the Federation see the Klingons as rivals and any connection to the high minded Federation ideals is quickly broken as far as they are concerned. And as the Organians find out, the Prime Directive, although the highest law in Federation jurisprudence, is not above a nudge and a wink as concerns indigenous peoples who might succumb to the benefits of dealing with the Klingons.

When the Organians prove to be a highly evolved race of "Aliens," and they ultimately prevent the Federation from killing Klingons, it is Kirk who yells the loudest and the longest. Kirk, the man on a mission of peace, is the most disturbed that he was ultimately prevented from killing Klingons and prevented from inducing the Organians to do the same.

During his dealings with the Organians Kirk offers them the benefits of Federation technology. He commits the same act of betrayal to the Prime Directive while dealing with the Capellens in another instance of conflicting interests with the Klingons. He is in effect attempting to make those indigenous "Aliens" more Federation like. One could argue that he is ultimately attempting to assimilate them.

When the Borg attempt to assimilate different species and cultures they are seen by the Federation as being evil. It never occurs to the members of the Federation and the Federation's henchmen at Starfleet, that the Borg are simply engaging in the same behavior as they themselves routinely do. Perhaps the source of conflict is that the Borg are better at the process.

The issue is not that assimilation is wrong as we have seen, it's that the Federation wishes to be the assimilator not the assimilatee. They would love to stop the Borg from doing their thing by doing *their* thing. It is an echo chamber of contradiction noiseless to Federation ears.

All of the aforementioned begs the question, what if there were no way to coexist with the Horta? What if it was an either-or situation and the Federation would have to leave all that precious pergieum? Would Kirk have spared the Horta in that case?

From: Dr. Flubdubulous [mailto: Ufale@napkin.net]
Sent: Friday August 20, 2004 2:35 AM
To: Tom Anderson

Subject: NYTimes Column

Did you read Frank Rich's column the other day? This article is the very definition of CRAP! Now I can add Frank Rich to my ever growing list of enemies. He actually said that Bush is a leader. And his argument that the war was unopposed by Democrats implies that the war is really their fault. I guess he didn't have enough space in his column to explain how it is actually the fault of Bill Clinton.

Perhaps Mr. Rich should go back to doing movie reviews. His complaint that the Dem.s ideas got no traction is ironic because I think their ideas for turning things around were good but the media guys found them boring so they didn't give them any attention other than on the day they were released.

Mr. Rich has angered me. I am so outraged I am going to put his name in the most hallowed spot on my enemies list, the space just below your name.

Best,

-----Original Message-----

From: Tom Anderson [mailto:Ufale@napkin.net]
Sent: Friday, August 20, 2004 5:54 AM
To: Dr. Flubdubulous
Subject: Re: NYTimes Column

I read that article. It essentially supports
all of the GOP's anti-Democrat talking points.
All Rich does is kick the can down the road.
He takes some banal criticism, and keeps it
afloat long enough for more saps to eat it up!
The real tragedy is that it probably took him
15 minutes to write it, and, he will take all
of these vacuous articles, and string them
together into a book.

_____

My Dearest Polly,

     It is very late here and as always my

thoughts are of you and your sister. I hope

she is well. I find my thoughts more and more

turning to those times when you and your sister

were children. When you both saw me as a

superhero rather than a flawed man. If I had a

choice on how I could spend eternity I would

pick those times. I could live there forever

and never tire.

You were a most remarkable child. That is a lucky thing a parent mustn't discount. The truth is, there is a certain amount of chance in the disposition and abilities a child may possess. You spin the wheel with every child you get. You could easily end up with a recalcitrant child who is a dullard. Or, as is the case with Uncle Tom, a cunning child of pure evil and malevolence.

The first few years of your life I continuously watched to see what kind of child you would be. I scrutinized every observation in my mind a thousand times over. I cross referenced every behavior, every interaction, every thing you said with all my knowledge of the world to glean what sort of person you were. I did it all with anticipation and with the dread fear you would be like your Uncle Tom.

I sensed that you were a perfect child but that did not stop me from watching you. I dreaded the thought that the evil genes which run in both mine and your mother's families would one day turn on and I would have to change your name to Darth Something.

The day I stopped worrying came in early spring when you were five years old. I got the idea to plant some trees in the front of the property to create a natural fence (the row of white pines you see there today) and I thought I could transplant some of the trees from the woods at the back of the property.

I took you with me in the blue Chevy truck. Long finger shaped shards of snow still gripped the ground refusing to give way to the warming spring air. Each tree and bush sported buds. The air was completely still.

I backed the truck up to the tree line and lifted you into the back of the truck so you could watch me and I could watch you. After I selected a quantity of small trees and it was

time to put them in the back of the truck I
took you out of the truck bed.

After a short while of loading I looked to
check on you and I saw you standing with your
hands clasped behind your back waiting
patiently for your crazy father to get done
with whatever inexplicable thing he was up to.
I can still see you, your hair in perfect
braids, wearing your little pink coat, standing
in an aura of perfect grace.

I knew then that I had nothing to worry
about and a great deal to live up to.

All my love

Daily Star-Home and Leisure Section D-*August 21, 2004*

Felonious Thoughts

Today's NYTIMES has a big article dissing the felony murder rule. Up till now I was on the fence about it but today I've decided. I propose we expand the felony murder rule to include everything. If you run a stop sign, cheat on your taxes, litter, steal, forget to bring back a library book on time, etc. it's the same as if you had killed someone. I know that the first thing you'll say is "ooooh but the prisons will be overcrowded!" That's true.

Under my proposal in a short while nearly all Americans will be doing time. The solution to that problem is easy. You enclose the entire continental United States with a 30 foot wall. The free population can live on Catalina Island and Hawaii (with room to spare).

The beauty of the "Felony Murder Wall of Justice" is that it will keep the prisoners in and the illegal immigrants out. It solves two big issues, the WAR on crime and illegal immigration, which appeals to all points on the political spectrum.

I am mindful that there are many smarty-pants lawyers who would gladly give me long, possibly boring, smarty-pants dissertations as to why I can't do what I am proposing. They'll cite precedent, dicta, and history. They'll probably mention all those who sacrificed and those who died to give us the legal rights I am proposing to throw away.

To the foolish naysayers with law degrees I say: "oh really?." I would cock one eyebrow when I said it. I would also tell them that we threw that all away when we agreed to Abu Garab, Guantanamo, waterboarding, military tribunals and so much more.

Mr. Bush and Company have transformed our legal system in very significant ways and very few people, many of whom would object to my idea, said anything about the matter.

Admittedly, the actions of the present administration may violate international law and they may (or may not) violate a few established U.S. laws. But isn't all that legal egghead stuff really just pretext to the matter of achieving fairness? Who can say if this system delivers less justice?

George Bush and his loyal minions have put a drive-through window on the justice system and my expansion of the felony murder rule just makes the service that much faster.

My expansion of the felony murder rule is very similar to the flat tax proposal offered up every election or so, in that it treats all criminals the same. What could be more fair than that? Did anyone ever go into court insisting that they be given less justice than the next guy?

I say, let justice be done! And thanks for your support.

Dr. Flubdubulous

_____

From: Dr. Flubdubulous [mailto: DrF@napkin.net]
Sent: Sunday, August 22, 2004 2:35 AM
To: Bruce Bauries Euphoria Pictures

Subject: Blood, Death and Sky

I just went through a knock down drag out fight with the computer technology here but I emerged victorious and with a top quality movie editing program. This program can do it all. You know what I'm gonna do? I'm gonna make "Blood Death & Sky" with my DVD handy cam. I intend to play all the parts myself. The only problem is I don't really know how to ride a horse so I'm gonna replace all the horses with motorcycles. I also have a problem with needles and getting my hands dirty so pizza will be used instead of the heroine (they have almost identical addictive properties) and my garage will be used instead of a real mine. Oh yeah, and since a location shoot in the Sonora desert is not in line with the budget I have to change the setting to Pennsylvania and oil to coal or possibly beer. But it will all be done artfully I can assure you. See you at the academy awards.

Diabetametrics: The Unreal Story of a True Superhero

Chapter 3

The day was cold. It was very cold and Howard liked it that way. He was never a big fan of winter but these past few months had changed a great many things. The blast of arctic air that hit him was real. The winter landscape with its flat colors and quiet demeanor seemed somehow engaging. There were aspects to it he'd never really seen or appreciated before.

Howard's opinions about many things had changed these past few months. His job was gone, his children were gone, his friends were gone and with them went his self respect. Sometimes he would sit in his chair in his home office and weep.

He trudged along, leaning slightly into the wind. His boots crunched the ice laid down from a storm that had hit two days ago. He heard nothing beyond the rhythmic crunching. Then, even that faded from his consciousness. All he had left were his thoughts.

He was thinking about the time his two daughters were young. These past few months he'd taken to long walks, wandering really, mostly thinking of them. There was not much else to do and staying in the house just made him feel worse.

His thoughts invariably took him to that time when they were all young, Lolly, he, and the girls. When he was strong and sure. When every thing he said was either wise or funny. When he had direction and a sense of self worth. When he was a hero.

The word hero bounced around his head for a bit. He used to play a game with the girls wherein he was Super-Dad and he would save them from the bad guys. He would take the blue oversized beach towel from the hall closet and don it as a cape. Once transformed, he would pick up the girls one in each arm, and fly them around the house. The flight to safety usually ended with them both being dumped squealing on either the couch or the big king sized bed in the master bedroom.

Howard made a left onto Carlton Avenue. Who was the Carlton this street was named after, he wondered. Does having a street named after you really have any meaning? It probably only mattered if one needed a good resume to get into heaven, he decided.

Having a street named after oneself was a manifestation of a system he'd been an unquestioning slave to his whole life. The pursuit of things. The amalgam of one's piece of the pie was the measure of oneself, the measure of happiness.

The Indian in the examination room painting probably owned ten things his whole life. He derived his happiness and sense of self worth from his loved ones and the world around him. He didn't attach his identity to some corporate entity or any semiannual evaluations. He didn't do it for the pay check, he did it for life.

It was obvious to Howard that he was being forced out when, after seventeen years of glowing evaluations, he suddenly received a terrible one. He could have sued, he could have gotten on the family leave act and/or dragged out his departure for a few years but in the end, he did nothing about the injustice done him. He requested an unpaid leave for health reasons and never went back.

The combination of his sickness and the heartbreaking blow to his pride at receiving an unsatisfactory report after giving so much to the company was too much for him to fight back. The system had bitchslapped him and all he could do was fall to the ground.

He was never good at confrontation. Perhaps he liked working with numbers because they had to follow rules. They were predictable. People were not. The vast intricacies of politics were unknown to him. Every set of rules had a set of unwritten rules that went with them and it seemed to Howard, that everyone was quite literate in reading the unwritten rules except him.

The world of nudge-nudge wink-wink, where much of human interaction took place, was beyond his comprehension. Howard dealt with his handicap in this area by working hard and not complaining. He coped by giving each employer way more than they gave him, by always telling the truth, and scrupulously abiding by the written rules.

A cold wind from the west bit into the right side of his face. Strangely, he didn't turn away from it. He just kept walking towards main street.

Howard started to recall all the jobs he had over his entire career. He thought of all the overtime, injuries, working lunches, sick days not taken. He calculated his approximate earnings for all that work and wondered where it had all gone.

It was all so much time wasted he thought. His intention was to build a future but it was more like building a sand castle by the ocean. It was only a matter of time before the ocean reached out with a wave and wiped it all out.

Still, it was an injustice. A galling injustice. An injustice the Indian would understand even though he didn't have Human Resources rules, social security and 401K's in his world. He'd understand completely the pain of losing all that meant anything to you. To have it ripped away for no valid reason.

Howard found himself at the corner of Carlton and Main. He couldn't remember walking the last half mile. He couldn't even say with any accuracy how long he'd been standing at the corner. The wind was harsher here, the openness of the main drag doing nothing to impede its flow.

There was a time when not remembering something would have bothered the hell out of him but now it was part of each day. More and more, the landscape of his mind seemed to be a fogged out mess. He made a mental note to work on it.

He turned left, not so that he could have the wind at his back but because he wanted to walk past the fire house and toward the library. He liked that portion of main street best because it was the part least altered since he was a child.

There was ice all along the edge of the road and numerous piles of blackened snow along the sidewalk but Howard's mind was brought to a summer day. He was sitting in the backseat of his father's station wagon the windows open, the acrid smoke from his father's cigarette spinning in the air before slipping out a window as they drove down this stretch of road.

It wasn't that he was hallucinating, it's just that the memory flashes could be intense. Howard let his mind play with the memory of that long ago day.

Nobody drives with the windows down anymore because they all have air-conditioning and nobody smokes anymore, he thought. When he was a boy all the parents smoked and nobody had air-conditioning except Doc the relatively wealthy pharmacist who drove a Cadillac so large you could make four modern day cars from it.

Doc was a good example of the adults of that era Howard mused. He was short, squat, and an angry, unrepentant disciplinarian. Doc yelled at and, or, cuffed any child that misbehaved in his store. It was a world run by adults for adults. Now world focus shifted to the children. A world for the children and woe be to any parent who didn't toe the line.

Even with his disdain for the new world of the child, Howard felt guilty for getting sick. He'd fallen apart just when they needed him most and he couldn't forgive himself for that. No matter how cogent the arguments he conjured in his mind for exoneration, he couldn't shed the guilt.

He looked up to see the bank on his left. It was the first built in his lifetime. All the other banks in town had been built long before he was born. Most of them were gone now. Maybe, he pondered, he'd do some business there as a means of paying them back for sticking around. Although what business he could not say since he was at the lowest economic point of his adult life.

He looked down and noticed that his gloveless hands were a purplish blue that did not look good. He thought about it for a moment and couldn't remember whether or not he'd put his gloves on before he left. Disturbing as that was, he reasoned that it didn't really matter and that the important point was to avoid frost bite. He resolved to swing by the library and head home from there.

He trudged on.

Chapter Six

Daily Star-Home and Leisure Section D-*September 4, 2004*

The Force of Profit

I always thought Obi Wan Kenobi was a bit of a loser. My opinion of him was based on the fact that even though he had tremendous power and abilities through his preternatural connection with the force, he had no material wealth. He didn't even have enough money saved to get a one way ticket for him and a couple of droids to Alderan. He had to convince a local yokel to sell his landspeeder to raise the funds.

As one who grew up in the lap of a society dedicated to over consumption and worshipful of profit, I couldn't understand how Obi Wan could eschew material wealth so thoroughly. It's true that one who is hiding out from the law shouldn't live too ostentatiously but there was nothing preventing him from squirreling away a few credits here and there over the years.

Now, as I see the insane amount of damage our glutinous lifestyle has reaped on our planet and ourselves I am beginning to understand the wisdom of old Obi Wan.

Obi Wan lived a simple life in pursuit of, among other things, long term happiness instead of short term pleasure. He didn't need a giant home to feed his ego while it drained his world of natural resources. He didn't require more material goods than he could possibly use in three lifetimes.

Although he never said it, he was living with the understanding that owning things is onerous. The things have to be cleaned, maintained, insured, and protected. Eventually, imperceptibly, the things enslave you. They rob you of the very freedom they were purported to provide.

Now, nearly 150 species of animals become extinct every day. In fifty years half of all the animal species on this planet will be gone, forever. Three billion more humans will add to the present six billion to take their place.

Of course, those three billion yet-to-be-borns will not live the luxurious lifestyle I wished Obi Wan to aspire to. That lifestyle is reserved for a very, very few on this planet. In order for every person on Earth to live as profligately as those in the first world nations do we would need eleven more planet earths.

I see now that I was wrong about Obi Wan. In my defense, I was raised to believe that a person's wealth was a measure of his worth and that profit is above all, a holy endeavor. The downside to this lifestyle choice was NEVER mentioned by anyone while I was growing up other than by a few persons referred to derisively as "Hippies."

Half of all the persons of first world nations who will die this year, will do so because they have too much fat around their hearts. Many of those will also have suffered from a nasty disease called diabetes which is caused mostly from an over consumption of high fructose processed foods. The foods that comprise the first world diet.

The lifestyle I wanted Obi Wan Kenobi to embrace, the one we've embraced whole heartedly, is killing us. It is decimating our health and the health of our planet.

Old Ben Kenobi, who lived out beyond the Dune Sea, is gone now. And even though I didn't hold with his ideas about the force, I do now see the value of living a simpler life. And now that it is apparent our lifestyle choices have had deadly effects, it seems, adopting Obi Wan's lifestyle is our only hope.

Dr. Flubdubulous

SPICER & MAHONEY

Military Surplus

Sir,

Enclosed you will fined one set of XG Mark IV night vision goggles $365.00. We value your patronage and have enclosed a Spicer and Mahoney catalogue for your convenience. Thank you.

From: Dr. Flubdubulous [mailto:DrF@napkin.net]
Sent: Sunday, September 5, 2004 6:46 PM
To: Tom Anderson
Subject: Car

```
What's all this crazy talk I hear that you

bought a standard shift car after I told you

not to during our phone conversation last week?

Say it isn't so, Joe.

Best,
```

From: Tom Anderson

Sent: Sunday, September 5, 2004 7:15 PM
To: Dr. Flubdubulous

Subject: Re: Car

FLASHBACK April, 1979.

A life altering moment of destiny. I nearly lost my life while replacing the points in my nine-year-old Toyota. My younger brother Andy was at the wheel, and I was at work over the engine compartment. Andy's job was simple...turn the key. I only needed him to crank the engine enough, so the distributor would be in the optimum position for the point gap. To my utter surprise, Andy neglected to keep the car in neutral. The result was the entire mass of the imported automobile being hurled towards me. My youth, and diet of heavily processed meats, was all that saved me from grievous harm. I nimbly flopped up on the fender as the vehicle fulfilled its ominous command.

The details surrounding this event are most painful for me to recall. Despite the threat to my health, I did not give up on standard shift cars, or irresponsible brothers. To save the environment, I bought a standard shift car just two days ago. The future is too important to me and I will not let my completely justified fear of this technology get in the way of the good of humanity.

Faithfully submitted...Your brother Tom, Victim, Martyr, Hero

On Sept 6, 2004, at 1:17 AM, Dr. Flubdubulous wrote:

There is no force in nature stronger than the attraction between bullshit and an old man's memories, and certainly nothing sweeter than self deception. I recall the incident you refer to. I was assisting you, instead of tending to my own concerns, and you did ask me to crank the engine. I remember checking the shift just before I turned the key. I shook it and although I was able to move it a good distance the car was in fact in first gear. As I was sure the car was in neutral, I saw no need to push in the clutch (modern day cars have a neutral safety switch which precludes one from making that mistake even if one is only fourteen and not attuned to the eccentricities of a TomShitMobile). When I cranked the engine the car did lurch forward. However, my quick reaction prevented it from actually rolling forward. I don't know that I would consider my quick reaction to the situation as actually saving your life but it is within eyesight of heroic.

I can understand how you would not include the pertinent facts in your account. After all, Viagra doesn't enhance one's ability to recall facts. And, as I have come to know, nothing can separate a feeble memory from comfortable delusions.

Best,

PS There is another connection here which I do not hesitate to make. The environmental concerns which you cite are baseless since the new automatic transmissions with locking torque converters are as efficient as standard transmissions. You purchased a standard shift car because you are trying to turn back the clock on technology. Yes, the man who once was ahead of everyone in technology use, e.g. Crystal Radio, CB Radio, Word Processor, Back Yard Weather Station etc., is now going Luddite. You are as much responsible for the very thing you are fighting against now as anyone. And now your war on technology has created a casualty. That is of course, your inability to use remote start. I guess it is true that Poetic Justice is the worst kind of hurt, huh?

From: Bruce Bauries Euphoria Pictures [mailto:
bbauries@hollywood.net]
Sent: Sunday, September 5, 2004 2:35 PM
To: Dr. Flubdubulous

Subject: Re: Blood, Death and Sky

```
Thanks for the notes on "Swingline."  I have
been considering cutting the ending to just one
funeral so as not to confuse the audience.


Blessings


PS Once we secure financing for "Swingline," we
will be sending you a fat check for all your
hard work.
```

Dr. F Replied September 5, 2004 7:20 PM EST

Believe it or not I had considered the multiple funerals
thing in "Swingline" but considered it a minor thing that
no one would notice by that point in the film. Audiences
can be quite willing to go along for the ride if they are
captivated by a good film i. e. the ridiculous ending in
Jaws. Still, they sound like good changes I shall await the
next draft.

Best,

Dr. F.

PS I have started a new book which will be of interest to
you and your partner. It's about the history of Euphoria
Pictures. Here's the best part, you don't have to do
anything to aid in its formulation. I have devised a

method of gathering information that doesn't require any time spent in actual interviews. This cutting edge technique utilizes a form of mathematics I call Suprasegmental Statistics. It's a blend of parametric and inferential statistics so complicated you have to be drunk just to understand its basics which, as fate would have it, I was when I conceived of it.

With Suprasegmental Statistics I can calculate with (reasonable) accuracy the answers you would give to any question I care to ask. This of course is only possible because as it happens the number of answers you can give to any question is finite and therefore knowable to statistical probability. I don't have to actually ask you a question to know the answer. In fact, I've already calculated what your response to this idea is already. But I digress.

This novel, titled "Euphoria Pictures: Truth in the Balance," is going to cover the entire history of Euphoria. It will include details of various production deals, behind the scenes stuff on "Road Blast," the illegitimate children, the prostitutes, all the nudity plus a detailed list of all the actors and producers that are considered enemies of Euphoria. There will be a an entire chapter dedicated to how Euphoria was the only production company in Hollywood that had the courage to accept money from Al Qaeda in the aftermath of 9/11. And much more.

It will be a four cornered truth fest worthy of the Pulitzer I'm going to turn down for it (Just because they're right doesn't give them the right to judge me!).

They say that Ben Franklin freed men by enlightening them. You're welcome.

```
Bruce Bauries Euphoria Pictures Replied:

Dude,

You're not going to list all the
prostitutes...?

B
```

GALACTICATION MAGAZINE, Issue 27 Vol. 2

REDEMPTION

By Dr. Flubdubulous

PART 4

SS Viper Command Ship of the first Imperial Fleet (IFF 1)

"What can you tell me of the boy Admiral?" Spivey rumbled.

It was the second time Captain Hock was summoned to speak with Spivey since the armada sailed and the War Master did not look pleased.

"Of course, I never met him personally," Hock started slowly. "I can only tell you what I know of him in battle."

"And what you've seen from your desk these past several circuits eh Hock?" Spivey sneered.

Hock ignored the insult and pressed on. "He doesn't fight conventionally when he can help it. He likes to use surprise-"

"Everyone likes to use surprise in warfare!" Spivey exploded. "Tell me something I don't know."

"Yes sir, I was getting to that, he has on occasion eschewed conventional tactics. He has split his forces several times, and once when completely outnumbered, at the Battle of Bandar, he placed all his ships in such close proximity to each other that he increased their shield strength tenfold. He then used them like a battering ram to disperse our forces and crushed them in turn."

"Yes, I remember reading about that one. Do you think he'll try that again?"

"I cannot say sir, however I do believe I know where he can be found."

"Where?"

"Along the frontier, near Falthor."

"Falthor? Why there? Because that is where his father was lost?"

"Yes and no, sir."

"What the hell does that mean?"

"Harmon prides himself on studying his enemy. He thinks that we will assume he wants revenge for his father so we will expect him there."

"You mean he wants to engage us?"

"Yes Sir."

"He's confident for one who is outnumbered."

"Yes Sir, but then, he's never lost a battle."

Hock could see that last comment did not sit well with Spivey. But then it didn't sit well with him either. The margin for error against a man like Harmon was indeed slim.

Command Ship Reach (C.S. 401k)

Plex blinked. He cleared his mind and blinked again. "Now do you understand?" Zach asked.

Plex nodded and looked out the viewport at the rest of the fleet streaking through space in sync with the Reach. The ships of so many various shapes and sizes looked more like a freight convoy than a fighting force. All had been hastily refitted with the latest weapons but until this latest moment he didn't realize the most dangerous weapon was standing next to him.

Zach had not only guessed that someone would divulge his battle plans from the Star Commander's office but he rightly anticipated that they might suffer from a credibility problem. He had the Norman fake reactor problems so that they could stay behind and send a second set of plans which made the first set look faked. It was a con game of the highest order.

"Whew! I understand but doesn't it hinge on their leader buying into the second set of plans? What if he just gets confused?"

"That is a possibility but it is blunted by the fact that he has twice our fighting force. He can either split his forces which would not be wise with the Targ being so new an ally, or pick one set of plans. He will not worry so much over the choice as he is confident."

"You know they've given command of their Armada to Spivey?"

"Yes, I know."

"He's no fool."

"I'm counting on that."

"So what is the real plan?" Plex asked as he turned back from the viewport.

"I'll release that only to our commanders just before the battle."

"That's cutting it close."

"Plex, this may not be easy for a Suh-Vak officer to hear but the only way I can ensure the loyalty of the commanders in those ships out there is through victory. It is also the only way I know of to keep as many of the crews in those ships alive as possible."

Command Ship Reach (C.S. 401k)

Zach sat at his desk with his eyes closed and his hands clasped in front of him. He was meditating. It won't be long now, he thought. History or humiliation.

"Admiral?"

"Yes" he said opening his eyes slowly.

"We are ready for your broadcast. All the commanders are standing by."

"Good, thank you."

He stood up and straightened his tunic. Then sat back down and flipped the switch to the vidscreen.

"Good Day to you all. I shall keep this message brief. In a very short while this battle will begin. Many of you may be doubtful of its outcome. I am not. We can, and will, be victorious. Just after we sailed each of you were given orders. You must now disregard those orders. At the end of this message you will be given orders which you must follow to the letter. There can be no deviation whatsoever without endangering our mission. Once you receive your orders you are to disable your communications systems. There will be no communications during battle. I have incorporated this detail into our plan because I know I can rely on all of you to follow your orders and I can trust you with my life."

He shifted in his chair slightly. He looked as if he were imparting something he really wasn't supposed to which of course heightened the attentions of those watching him. "Friends, together we have fought and suffered through many years of war. It ends today. Good luck and Good hunting."

The vidscreen went black and Zach turned to Pask.

"Send them."

Fighting Ship Valiant (F.S. 2308)

Julie Bedford reached for the vidscreen and turned it off. She stared at it for a moment deep in thought. New orders.

"It looks like you were correct Pleat. The battle will be at Falthor. What can you tell me about it? I was still in the Middle Academy when the Battle of the Frontier took place."

Pleat cleared his throat and said, "Falthor is essentially a large rock. It is indistinguishable from all the other sub-planetoid sized rocks in space except that it never moves. It is held in place by intersecting ripples of gravity emanating from the Frontier."

So the Admiral wants to fight an armada twice his size near a section of space bounded by that insidious Frontier, she thought. His men were right about him. They didn't *say* the Frontier but everything they'd told her added up to this. Lucky for the Admiral they work for him and not the Vicassians.

She leaned over and snapped a button on the consol below the vidscreen. "How long before we reach Falthor?"

"Sir, we should be on station in two eights," a low voice emanated from the comm speaker.

Two eights, that was not much time. She looked at Pleat and could read his thoughts. This was the moment of truth. Was she going to side with her officers or her lawful orders?

She did not take her eyes off of Pleat. There was something unspoken in their gaze. She hit the comm switch on her desk. "Have all senior officers meet me in the conference room on the double."

"Yes Sir," came the reply.

"Well Mr. Pleat, let us go meet with our co-conspirators."

"Yes, Captain," he said smiling for the first time since she'd met him.

```
> -----Original Message-----
From: Dolly Anderson [mailto:kittygrl@napkin.net]
Sent: Monday, September 6, 2004 9:30 AM
To: Sue Green
Subject: Lunch

Sue,


I'm sorry but I can't make lunch this Thurs.
Andy has been acting somewhat irrational lately
and I'm afraid to leave him alone.

Dolly
```

Irrational how? Is he wetting his pants?

Drooling? Eating dog food? What?

Sue,

Dolly Anderson Replied 9/6/04 11:00 AM EST

He disappears in to the woods for hours at a
time. He says he's on patrol. When he is home
he spends the majority of his time looking out
the windows to "Watch the avenues of approach."
(He claims a turtle tried to chew through the
phone cable in an effort to "disrupt
communications.") He refuses to cut the grass
because, he says, "That's exactly what the
enemy wants." Apparently, tall grass limits
the visibility of enemies that are not so tall.

That kind of irrational.

I've tried all the ways I know to reach him but
nothing seems to work. I'm afraid to leave him
alone.

Dolly,

Are we still on for next Sunday? If so, please
mail me some gas money. You know...for the
extra mileage required for my journey.

From: Dr. Flubdubulous [mailto:DrF@napkin.net]
Sent: Monday, September 6, 2004 6:45 PM
To: Tom Anderson
Subject: Re: Kittatiny

Now I feel bad about not being able to meet

with you this weekend. I had a vision today.

I don't have them often so when I do, they mean

a lot. In my vision you and I were playing air

hockey and I was beating you without the mercy

you don't deserve. After I beat you with a

score of seven to one and after I waited for

you to stop crying, we played that hockey game

you always cheated at. You know . . . the one

that you manipulate the players with the

turning knobs? I beat you five to zero. I was

a scoring machine. I didn't just play the game

I became *of* the game. And that's the saddest

part of not being able to meet with you this

weekend. I have to skip the sweet victories

which would have taught you a valuable lesson

and provided me with an unending source of amusement for decades to come. Well such is life and such was my vision. I'm sorry I had to humiliate you and then not humiliate you by not showing up. The only thing worse than fate is knowing one's fate. Until next time . . .

Best,

_____

-----Original Message-----

From: Dr. Flubdubulous [mailto:DrF@napkin.net]
Sent: Monday, September 6, 2004 7:10 PM
To: Bruce Bauries Euphoria Pictures
Subject: Brilliantly Brilliant

I came up with a brilliant idea. In fact, its so good I'm not sure I should tell you. I'm gonna have to think about it, hold on . . . . Okay, thanks for waiting. Here goes, "Make Your Own God." All your life you've had gods of all descriptions and functions shoved at you by everybody. Well maybe its time for you to shove back. You design your god, you give it gender, purpose, powers, taboos . . . whatever you want. You place the order and for a small fee, I'll make the physical manifestation of your personal contribution to the cosmos in my "Celestial Manufacturing" facility located at the end of the "Eternal Driveway" behind my house. I was thinking of calling my company, "Gods in a Garage" or "Blasphemy Incorporated" or "Gods R You." Whatever the name of my corporation you're guaranteed to get the god you want. Maybe you want a god of truth or perhaps you want a god of a more eclectic flavor such as the god of fertility and beer (two things I have found to be inextricably linked) or the god of tuna fish and mayonnaise. It's all up to you! And, since it's your own creation, you'll be the only person on your block to have one! Think about it.

Best,

Dr. F

PPS Due to shipping concerns no god can be bigger than five and a half feet tall or weigh more than 70 pounds.

From: Bruce Bauries Euphoria Pictures
[mailto:DrF@napkin.net]
Sent: Monday, September 6, 2004 9:21 PM
To: Dr. Flubdubulous
Subject: Re: Brilliantly Brilliant

I like it.

_____

Deceptively Simple

One of my biggest problems is that I have never been comfortable with deception. I have practiced it, sometimes with abandon and other times with reticence but I have never felt right doing so.

It is a sad lonely existence when you cannot be dishonest–on earth anyway. I would like to believe that there is a planet of flawless honesty somewhere out there in the vastness of space. I think, although honest measure may contain barbs, that world would ultimately be soothing, comfortable and infinitely desirable for someone like myself–the lying impaired.

As anyone who has read this column will tell you, I am committed to truth. I don't like truth nor do I like the arduous task of obtaining it but I am as committed to labor in its service as I am to breathing. It is a struggle of necessity.

In the dawn of man, truth was a matter of survival and rather straight forward. The best survival strategy one could have in those days was to cling to truth. Truth was relegated to a less honored roll with the rise of the state. Industrialization forced truth to occupy such a small slice of daily life it's own mother wouldn't recognize it.

Truth simply doesn't work much in the arrangement of the modern industrial state. Deception plays such a large roll in the day to day operations, truth simply doesn't have much to do. Ironically, the mass media, fully capable of reaching everybody, has less use for truth than a fat prom dress does.

First and foremost of the media are advertisers. They provide the profits and thereby the existence of the media. The last thing they want is truth anywhere in the mix. They adhere to the fundamental truth that one can never sell useless and overpriced goods by calling them as such.

Entertainment and news, often one and the same, similarly have little use for the truth other than to use a small portion of it as a shiny veneer for their wares. Politicians, pundits and the public avoid truth as if it were a pair of cactus style proctology gloves.

You could, as many have, call me a fool for having such beliefs. You could point out that advocating for that which will only jam the gears of the modern society is pure madness. However, that is a truth I'm prepared to live with.

Just because deception has been so thoroughly woven into the fabric of our lives does not mean we are obligated to wear it blindly.

Dr. Flubdubulous

_____

"The Case for Darth Vader"

In Luke Skywalker's first lesson on the ways of the force, Obi Wan Kenobi instructs him to "let go your conscious self," and the reason he does so is because that is how the Jedi sell their version of the force. They require one to give up all reason in order to accept their outrageous perversion of the facts.

They start out by framing the matter as a two sided issue: light or dark. If your not with em your agin em. One cannot be, as young Anakin Skywalker was, open minded about what the force truly is. To the Jedi and their ilk, light is light, dark is dark, and never the twain shall meet.

The prophecy stated that Anakin Skywalker was to bring balance to the force and the Jedi immediately seized upon this as meaning that he would some day murder the Sith whose identity they claimed not to know at the time Anakin was set on the path they wished him to take. It never occurred to them that young Mr. Skywalker with his preternatural connection to the force might one day bring balance to the force by joining both the light and the dark sides into a harmonizing blend that would uplift the Republic.

The evidence shows that Anakin Skywalker was abused and exploited by the high toned Jedi to further their aggressive and shameful grab at power. Anakin was maimed and defamed by them and was only restored to their good graces after he committed homicide and treason for them.

Anakin Skywalker's odyssey begins when he was found to have an exceptional connection with the force. The Jedi Knight Qigong Jin discovered Anakin on Tattoine and was struck by how Anakin seemed to have a strong relationship with the force. In typical Jedi fashion, Qigong takes a blood sample to test Anakin's midiclorion levels under false pretenses. He does not answer Anakin's question as to what he is doing honestly, nor does he seek permission from Anakin's mother.

Qigong learns through his underhanded, dishonest, unethical physical examination of Anakin, that Anakin has an unusually high midiclorion count. After meditation over this fact and after a conversation with Anakin's mother wherein it is revealed she is not sure how she came to be pregnant with Anakin, Qigong determines that Anakin is going to be the one prophesied to bring balance to the force.

Prior to discovering the value Anakin had to the Jedi, Qigong was content to let Anakin and his mother live out their lives as slaves on a harsh and violent planet. However, once Qigong realizes that Anakin is suitable fabric for a Sith-killer he arranges to have him released from slavery. Ever mindful of the bottom line, Qigong arranges to have Anakin earn the money needed for his emancipation by risking Anakin's life in a deadly Pod race.

Anakin's mother has no real value to the Jedi so she is left to wallow in servitude and is convinced to render onto the Jedi the one thing of value to her in the whole universe, her only son. Even though Qigong and his loyal sidekick Obi Wan have fantastic powers which exceed most living beings in their galaxy of long ago, neither of them can conjure up a means of liberating Anakin's mother. And even though they are traveling with a Queen of an entire planet they have not the resources to help Anakin's mother.

Once Anakin was transferred from one form of slavery to another, the Jedi never return to help his mother. In fact, Obi Wan Kenobi returns to Tattoine approximately ten years after leaving with Anakin, yet he doesn't attempt to contact Anakin's mother. He changes his name to Ben, most likely in an attempt to

throw off any creditors searching for him, and
spends the next two decades living as a hermit
out beyond the Dune Sea.

Anakin's mother is eventually purchased by
a moisture farmer and "marries" him. Their
"marriage" produces a son, Owen.
Unfortunately, Anakin's mother is kidnapped by
some bad men and tortured. Broken and beaten,
as she slips toward eternal night, she gets the
one thing she has longed for since the day the
Jedi led her son away, she sees Anakin. Her
joy at their reunion is extinguished by the
fact that she was late for the grave and she
would rather her beloved son not see her in
that condition.

A poor woman who has been abused,
enslaved, raped and left for dead, Anakin's
mother finally leaves her pains behind. There
was not one Jedi present beside Anakin when she
passed.

The Jedi rigorously train Anakin to bring "justice" to the universe. Their justification for being is to keep the peace yet they frequently approach any given situation with an air of menace and always armed. Anakin is told time and again that he is to keep his light saber with him at all times. He is in effect told that his life is dependent upon his ability to do violence.

From the time the Jedi removed him from his home and brought him to Couricsant for training so that he might serve them better, the only person who showed any real interest in Anakin was Emperor Palpatine, then Senator from Nabu. It is easy to argue that as a Sith Lord the Emperor's interest was similar if not the same as the Jedi as concerns the boy with the stronger than strong connection to the force, however, the Emperor waited till Anakin was at the age of consent before offering the benefits of the "Dark" side.

Palpatine offers Anakin respect by appealing to his intellect, something the Jedi failed to do by consistently expressing complex issues in terms of dichotomous variables. Palpatine tells Anakin that, "Good is a point of view." Anakin begins to understand the subjective nature of good and evil when the Jedi, beings whom he always assumed were solidly on the side of good, begin to rationalize negative behaviors such as lying, spying, and treason.

Anakin is told not to interfere when he encounters the Jedi Death Squad on its way to the Supreme Chancellor's office to fulfill its dirty mission. He attempts to communicate rationally with Mace Windu, the lead hit man. Anakin offers to go with Master Windu to help mediate the situation so that violence is not necessary but Mace orders Anakin to stay put as he has no intention of letting kindness or reason stop him from what he intends to do.

The violent confrontation with Supreme Chancellor Palpatine is solely the product of Jedi rage. Their decision to escalate the conflict to the realm of violence forces Anakin to decide to join with the Chancellor and become a Sith Lord. He casts off the yoke of the Jedi and becomes Darth Vader.

It is clear from the evidence that Anakin's decision to "go over to the Dark Side," is the correct one. He refuses to turn against the government and personally ends the separatist war by going to the Mustafar system.

Upon learning that Anakin Skywalker has become Darth Vader, Yoda, without hesitation, tells Obi Wan Kenobi that he must kill Darth Vader. Obi Wan hesitates at the prospect for all of thirty seconds then sets out to kill his former Padawon for breaking with the faith.

After tricking Padmay into revealing the location of the newly minted Sith Lord, Darth Vader, Obi Wan maims him and leaves him for

dead. Just before he leaves however, he tells
Vader, "I loved you like a brother!" We can
infer from this that perhaps "Jedi love" is the
most fleeting of all.

Ultimately it is Emperor Palpatine who
saves Darth Vader. While he is saving Vader
via use of his medical droids the Jedi are
stealing Vader's children and separating them
so that they may be better hid from their
father.

Although it may seem that giving the male
child Luke to Vader's half-brother Owen is not
a class "A" job of hiding a child, the method
seems to have worked. Vader does not learn of
his son until he is told about him many years
later by Palpatine. Palpatine also offers to
train Luke in the ways of the "Dark" side.

Of course by that time, the Jedi already
have their hooks in Luke. They had already
convinced him to join their ranks and arranged
the rank of Commander for him with the rebel

forces seeking to destroy the Empire his father worked so hard to help build.

As with his father, Luke's introduction to the Jedi begins with lies. Obi Wan tells him that his father was betrayed and murdered by Darth Vader, a good pupil till he turned to the "Dark" side. He also tells Luke, as he hands him a light saber, that his father wanted him to have it, implying that his father was aware of his existence.

Luke is so brain-washed by the Jedi that when his father, a Sith Lord, tells him the truth the Jedi specifically worked to keep him from, he travels back to Yoda for confirmation. Yoda, realizing that the truth is out, finally admits that Vader is indeed Luke's father.

When Luke, who is understandably dismayed that the Jedi lied to him, confronts Obi Wan about his lies, Obi Wan explains that what he'd said was not so much a lie as it was a prevarication. He tells Luke that, "What I told you was true, from a certain point of view." The view of a Jedi.

Obi wan, the Master Jedi, the one who is not supposed to be evil like a Sith Lord, attempts to convince Luke to commit premeditated patricide. Luke, to his credit, refuses and Obi Wan says, "Then the Emperor has already won."

Obi Wan's reaction to Luke's refusal to kill his own father is a naked attempt to pressure him into doing the deed he tried to accomplish so many years before when he maimed and burned Darth Vader.

The Jedi tell Luke over and over that anger and hatred lead one to the dark side but are those so called negative emotions really negative? Channeling aggression fear and hatred is preferable to denial. One can hate poverty, and be angry over injustice. Certainly those emotions are not incompatible with the high minded tones of the Jedi.

The last words a broken and demoralized Vader speaks convey a belief that Luke was right about him. Luke said there was good in him and indeed there was. Which begs the question, are Sith Lords evil? After all, many of the truths we cling to depend on a certain point of view.

-----Original Message-----
From: Dr. Flubdubulous [mailto:DrF@napkin.net]
Sent: Wednesday, September 8, 2004 3:45 AM
To: Tom Anderson
Subject: Sit Rep

As to defense spending, if you were responsible for increasing defense spending with no questions asked these past few years would have surpassed your fondest dreams by a few light years. No questions asked!

Best,

PS I was watching all the old Battlestar Gallactica episodes and I was amazed at how many of the bad guys were former bad guys on Star Trek. The recidivism rate among Klingons is shockingly high. Somebody needs to do something.

From: Tom Anderson [mailto:Ufale@napkin.net]
Sent: Wednesday, September 8, 2004 4:15 PM
To: Dr. Flubdubulous
Subject: Re: Sit Rep

These comments disturb me. Either Andy is

working on his new tell-all book about life, or

he is just plain drunk as hell. The smart

money is on both.

Tom

On Sept. 8, 2004 9:02 PM, Dr. Flubdubulous <Dr.F@napkin.net> wrote:

Thank you for your prompt reply. I know how much you dislike facts (especially those of your past). I should remind you that drunk or not, I am always a loyal servant of truth. A fact which should hold no influence over any man who's past is well acquitted.

Best,

PS The situation in Iraq is worse than all possible predictions. It seems now the insurgents are making so much money off the dismal situation there that they are actually engaging in foreign operations. What price the 2000 election?

PPS My wife related your phone message from the other day. It is most unfortunate that I must decline your semi-gracious invitation to spend slightly more than twenty four hours at your house this weekend. I'm afraid it is not the will of Allah. It would be an unconscionable insult to propriety were I to neglect to thank you for your almost decent offer.

Chapter Seven

From: Dr. Flubdubulous [mailto: DrF@napkin.net]
Sent: Friday, Oct. 1, 2004 2:38 AM
To: Bruce Bauries Euphoria Pictures

Subject: Movie Ideuh

You know how they always have TV shows and movies about killer asteroids? Well what if a not so killer asteroid came our way? Suppose scientists discover an asteroid of not so large a size to destroy the earth but could do a bunch of damage to the surrounding area of where it hits, is on its way to earth. Suppose the Space Agency in charge of such things actually has the technology to move the asteroid off course and miss the earth completely. No problem, right? But the accountants have done the math. They've covered all the angles. They've accurately determined that China, despite its lame-o government, is in ascendancy, the U.S. is in decline. Nothing can stop China from being the premiere economic and military power in twenty years. Unless . . . unless an asteroid of just the right size (the bad guys dub the asteroid Goldilocks) plows into central China. The handsome young hero, Dr. Flubdubulous (working name) finds out and has to stop the bad guys from doing their worst. Throw in an evil scientist, a few nude scenes, a car chase or two, and you've got yourself a hit. You're welcome.

From: Tom Anderson [mailto:Ufale@napkin.net]
Sent: Friday, October 1, 2004 9:03 AM
To: Dr. Flubdubulous
Subject: Sunrise

The story that you told me today is extraordinary! One four year old crossing a four lane highway is shocking by today's standards. Add a three year old and a two year old to the mix, and you have a situation that is unimaginable. Was that the way that things were done back then? Or, were we considered low-lifes in our own low-life neighborhood?

Also, where the hell could you have possibly been going? Wasn't everything that you needed on the south side of Sunrise?

From: Dr. Flubdubulous [mailto:DrF@napkin.net]
Sent: Friday, October 1, 2004 10:23 AM
To: Tom Anderson
Subject: Sunrise

Sometimes when I sit down and think about some of the ways we lived back then I get a feeling of anxiety. A feeling, although not in the same measure, akin to the feeling I got when I was nearly killed in my back yard. I suppose such rumination serves little purpose.

I was four years old when I crossed Sunrise Hwy with Brandon and Steve. I think we were going

over to the school to play on the equipment but
I don't believe we actually made it there. I
think we decided to go back. Charlie the floor
waxer did see me and told mom. She yelled at
me when I got home. Of course my thinking as a
parent is that one should never punish or
berate children for acting like children. If
you fail to properly supervise four year olds
they will do things that won't always meet with
your satisfaction. It won't surprise you to
know however, that in subsequent years mom has
often told this story as me being the villain.
In more than a few retellings of this story mom
referred to me as "this dope" or "this dope
over here."

I have no doubt there were a few folks in our
neighborhood who looked down on us. But who
could blame them. On the other hand I don't
recall a whole lot of slaves to virtue in the
vicinity.

Go figure.

Best,

_____

Diabetametrics: The Unreal Story of a True

Superhero

Chapter 5

Somehow salt tasted saltier to Howard and he began
adding it to his food. Now, the paltry amount of food he was
permitted was mostly substitutes for real food. Tofu dogs instead

of the beef franks he loved so dearly, rice cakes instead of bagels, nothing instead of most things.

Howard mourned the loss of these things and more and more, the melancholy grew. It seeped into every room in his psyche. It began to pervade and weigh down his entire outlook until it came to feel as if he was mourning the death of a loved one.

He told himself that it was all silliness. He reasoned that he should just forget it all but the bad feelings kept tugging at him. They were relentless.

Howard looked around the room. He had spent years of his life in rooms like this. Once the years were safely in the past, it was as if the experience never happened, and yet, they had happened. The lines on his face, his graying hair, and other various problems served as testimony to them. The exigencies and as Howard saw them, the indignities, of age wouldn't let him forget the years.

But the memories themselves were darker and dimmer now. The day to day stuff was completely gone and what remained of the highlights was almost like a scrambled porn channel. Bits and pieces now and again with a provocative moment obscured quickly. Thankfully, the memories of the girls remained mostly in tact.

The room was illuminated with overly bright fluorescent bulbs. And as if that were not enough, there was an abundance of reflective surfaces. Gleaming steel and polished porcelain stabbed at his retinas so forcefully that he wished he'd brought sunglasses.

It wasn't the pain of the lights or the arrangement of the furniture or even the vague smell of antibacterial soap, which seemed impossible to ignore, that bothered Howard. He was bothered by how unnatural it all was. He'd spent so much of his life in rooms so unnatural.

"Sit still," Lolly said.

"I am still. The world is moving."

"Ha, ha."

"Yes, I do think that is very Ha, ha, as you say."

Lolly was with him because ever since that day he'd gotten the news from the Doctor, he didn't wish to interact with the medical community alone. He didn't trust his perceptions with them. They seemed to speak a different language.

Medical personnel are prone to say things like, "You'll feel a little pinch," or "You're gonna feel a little pressure," or "It's treatable." Even more confounding was that they always used his first name and said it with five more decibels than was required. They used a tone and volume which suggested they were under the impression they were in fact tasked with trying to talk him off of a high ledge rather than providing medical care.

"He went to the river. The river was there," Howard said.

"What? What does that mean?" Lolly turned to stare at him.

"Nothing, it's something I read once. I always liked it even though I never really felt I knew what it meant." Howard reflected on the sentiment for a moment then added with a chuckle, "It's a bit like life."

Just then, a short squat woman in a lab coat entered. Howard's brain perceived her as a series of shapes, round head, square body, cylinders for arms and legs, square feet. She lumbered directly toward them. She had short orange hair.

Howard marveled at how unhuman this human looked. She seemed more like a transport device for fat cells than an independent person capable of independent thought. Howard felt a little sorry for her, even though she was a card carrying, needle wielding member of the medical establishment.

"Hiya Howie. How are we today?"

"Fine today, thank you," he said, his pity rapidly drying.

"Just today?"

"Today I am fine. I won't hazard a guess about tomorrow."

She laughed a jiggly laugh and Howard judged it a genuine laugh based on the moving flab coefficient.

"Why don't you come with me and we'll check your blood."

Inwardly Howard shivered, outwardly he rose and followed the large phlebotomist. Howard dubbed her the phlebotomist with the biggest bottomist on their way to the blood drawing area.

✦✦✦✦✦✦✦✦✦✦✦

The smooth green water of the Great South Bay became lightly choppy and slowly turned into a rich cobalt blue the closer they got to the inlet. It seemed to have a steely, deep quality that implied such tremendous strength that Howard took a deep breath. The salt air stung his nose slightly. He looked to his left and could see the Fire Island lighthouse. It was made with nearly one million bricks and its lower walls were twelve feet thick Howard recalled.

He stared at the lighthouse while he searched his mind for where he'd picked up that information. Then it came to him. It had been on a third grade field trip. He couldn't recall the teacher's name or the names of anyone else except Paul, a friend. Paul was a good kid with a great deal of potential but he died of leukemia in the sixth grade.

The thought of Paul and his shorter than short life gave Howard pause. He realized he should be grateful for the time he had, and feeling cheated out of the promise of his golden years was almost blasphemous in light of what Paul had lost. It was logical, and an acceptable fact of life, that some people had it better and some people had it worse. Howard told himself that one more time before he turned away from the object of so many field trips, but it didn't help.

He looked out over the bow of the lurching boat at the inlet. He could see the Atlantic ocean on the other side. They were heading out to do some fishing. The thought of killing fish depressed him. It repulsed him. Killing something healthy seemed absurd. Stealing so precious a commodity as health, something time would do eventually, seemed incredibly wrong.

A burst of cold air hit Howard's face and the bright sunlit inlet and the ocean beyond dissolved into a gun metal gray morning on Main street. He was trudging into the wind again. Bits of icy snow blowing down from the heavy overcast bit into his cheeks.

How many years had it been since Paul died he wondered. How many more years did he get than Paul? How did Paul cope with dying so early in life? How did any of them cope? The young ones. The ones who had it all striped away before . . . before payment was due.

Howard could hear children playing. The noise grew, expanding to fill all the sounds on the spectrum. It was another memory. The school yard fifth grade. Howard was standing near the goal line when a football wobbled past his feet. On an impulse, he reached out with his right foot and touched the ball as it passed. It was a light touch and did nothing to alter the ball's intended direction or speed.

A short kid, the over competitive type, came running up to Howard screaming obscenities. He shoved Howard but before he could attack, Paul was between them. Paul, who hadn't been much of a friend since the third grade, was now being the peace maker, something unheard of at that school.

In his mind's eye Howard could see Paul handling the dispute as well as any adult could have. Now that Howard was an adult, Paul's curious behavior that day is much less of a curiosity. Now, it was clear that Paul, in that short span of time between diagnosis and death, was forced to become an adult. He had to cover a great distance in an undersized period.

Howard wondered what insights a child at Paul's age could have developed at the last. He certainly had more time to contemplate than Paul ever got, and had more life experience to work with.

Howard smiled at the thought of time to think. These past few months, as an exile in his own country, he'd had plenty of time to consider the longer questions. Howard came to believe, through all his musings, that most of the things he valued were of very little value. Having a respectable job, a nice home and tons of stuff meant nothing. Even having a squeaky clean lawn mower that cut the lawn perfectly was, in the large scope of reality, meaningless.

Howard's conclusions shamed him. He felt guilty for having focused his life on stuff rather than his family. He consoled himself with the thought that at the time, he believed he was doing right by his family. Providing them with stuff was supposed to bring them happiness. Doctrine he'd never questioned until recently.

Then his thoughts turned to his own happiness. All the stuff had ultimately brought him very little happiness. The material wealth put such demands on his time in their care and maintenance that it almost seemed Howard that *they* owned him. He tried to calculate how much time he spent in service to his stuff instead of with his family but even with his better than average accounting skills it was impossible.

Howard gave up and decided to check where he was. He was at the library. He considered going in but changed his mind because he didn't believe he had the energy to be polite to the ladies at the front desk.

He headed for home.

-----Original Message-----
From: Dr. Flubdubulous [mailto: DrF@napkin.net]
Sent: Friday, October 1, 2004 10:45 AM
To: Bruce Bauries Euphoria Pictures

Subject: Movie Thoughts

Do you believe in omens? It's not very scientific but lately I've been giving them a great deal of thought. Yesterday I came up with an idea about a baby sentenced to life in prison and today there is an editorial in the NYTimes about how we should not put juveniles in adult prisons. Now that is fate waving a freshly peeled onion right under my nose.

I read a book by a guy who wrote books and then died. Ordinarily I don't have any respect for anyone stupid enough to die but his book kinda made sense. He said that the worst time when writing a novel is when you just get past one hundred pages. If your charge falters for any reason you'll lose the magic and never make it up that hill. I am just at that point in a novel that is so novel, so eccentric, so bizarrely original, they will either name a university after me or have me executed by firing squad for having written it. So maybe I'm just looking for a way out. On the other hand, it doesn't pay to turn a deaf ear when the cosmos comes aknockin. Maybe it is one's reading comprehension as concerns omens that determines their fate. Who knows?

Best,

Dr. F

PS You should know that as Admiral of Production for Euphoria East's blockbuster production of Blood, Death and Sky: the Pennsylvania edition, I had to make several script changes. Due to a lack of firearms, the scenes encompassing same have been altered. The actors were issued calculators and the story amended to be that they are all accountants. Lines like "Don't move or I'll shoot you." Have been changed to "Don't move or I'll have you audited!" and so on. And all those characters who were shot to death in the original script, merely receive a savage beating with textbooks on double entry book keeping in the latest version.

From: Bruce Bauries Euphoria Pictures
Sent: Friday, October 1, 2004 11:41 AM
To: Dr. Flubdubulous

Subject: Re: Movie Thoughts

I love those changes to B,D&S. But tell
me, how do we deal with the issue of the
Tesla coil? I mean, Tesla was a most
unaccountable genius.

On Oct 1, 2004 9:02 AM, Dr. Flubdubulous DrF@napkin.net> wrote:

I have solved the dilemma of the
Tesla Coil. I figured that since
most people have never seen a Tesla
coil and most of the interior scenes,
due to budget considerations, have to
be shot in my garage, all I needed
was an unusual looking machine that
could fit in my garage. My late
Father-in-law was a petit' Tesla.
Along with some very curious opinions
of "da Jews" he possessed a felicity
with all types of metal. He designed
and built, mostly from old garbage
truck parts he took from his last
job, a can crusher. I took the can
crusher added a set of jumper cables,
duct taped a couple of motorcycle
batteries in strategic locations and
perched a five gallon water bottle on
top. It looks so much like what an
audience would expect a Tesla Coil to

look like, my Father-in-law himself
wouldn't recognize it. God rest his
thieving, anti-Semitic soul.

Best,

Dr. F.

  -----Original Message-----
From: Dr. Flubdubulous [mailto: DrF@napkin.net]
Sent: Friday, October 1, 2004 10:55 AM
To: Tom Anderson
Subject: Media and Mass Murder

I think the entire media industrial complex has
broken down. It's not doing what it should. It's like
the band in "Animal House," continuing to march
into a wall without contemplating the absurdity of
their actions. Search your feelings, you know it to
be true!

Best,

PS Question: How do you commit mass murder
and get away with it? I'm talkin get away clean?
Answer: Open a McDonald's. Ray Kroc killed way
more people than Hitler ever dreamed of, yet very
few would put both in the same historical
classification. Put that in your McHistory books
and teach it in your McSchools and maybe I'll
respect you.

From: Tom Anderson [mailto: Ufale@napkin.net]
Sent: Friday, October 1, 2004 3:45 PM
To: Dr. Flubdubulous
Subject: Re: Media and Mass Murder

This thing with the Turtle is getting out of hand. Get some help! We should meet.

On Oct 1, 2004 9:02 AM, Dr. Flubdubulous DrF@napkin.net> wrote:

This is not the time to meet. I don't need "help" as you put it. I am of sound mind. What I need is luck, an indispensable component of any successful endeavor. Instead of questioning my sanity, you could and should be wishing me well

Best,

PS What about a Hallmark Hall of Fame movie about an Assistant Principal who goes hunting to relieve the stress of being an underpaid public school employee and accidentally kills a unicorn. Naturally, he is upset about the accident and in his grief he finds that not only was it the last unicorn but it was the unicorn that saved his father's life during the war. When questioned by his family he has not the courage to admit what he did. He lies to them. The Assistant Principal decides to go for a drive to relieve the pressure he feels over the accident and lying to his family. While driving through the most picturesque mountain range he has ever seen, the Assistant Principal accidentally runs over a Leprechaun. The Leprechaun was out picnicking with his family celebrating the advent of his retirement. The most tragic part of the accident was that the dearly departed Leprechaun was about to tell his family where his pot of gold was hidden just before he was turned into bumper meat. Now the Assistant Principal's life had taken a severe turn for the worse. He is being sued by various environmental lobbyists for killing the last unicorn and he is being sued by the ACLU for violating the Civil Rights of the Leprechaun. Seriously depressed, he sees no way out of his predicament. He finally decides to run away to sea. He joins the Merchant Marine and several weeks later he is found lying on a beach completely dead. He had been beaten to death by a gang of angry mermaids. The moral of the story here is that you cannot solve your problems by lying or running away.

PPS I will have Spivey or he will have me.

From: Daily Star Feedback
[mailto:dlystrfdbk@broadstream.net]

Sent: Saturday, October 2, 2004 10:30 AM

To: Dr. Flubdubulous

Subject: FW: FEEDBACK

Have you every thought of using a gun idiot!

*****

My 12 year old son and I read you column faithfully. We have disagreed as to what Spivey represents. I say he is evil and my son says he is our war in Iraq. Please let us know which, if either, of us is correct. There is a pizza riding on your answer.

*****

Daily Star-Home and Leisure Section D-*October 2, 2004*

Falling Fate

If a tree falls in the forest and no one is there to hear it, does it make a sound? The way you answer that question, whether or not anyone is around to hear you answer that question, speaks volumes about your personal philosophy as to the nature of existence.

If you say you believe the fallen tree makes a noise your are in effect saying that you believe that what transpires in the universe is wholly independent of man's existence. However, if you say that no noise is derived from the fallen tree, then you are saying, in essence, that if it doesn't have anything to do with mankind, it didn't happen.

I know that this fundamental question has been asked, thought about, and answered by humans for many centuries but I wonder, did anyone ever ask about the tree itself? Was it old and sick? Was it horribly depressed and so committed suicide? Was it young and in love when tragedy struck?

I wasn't thinking any thoughts of philosophy or cosmology when I heard a tree fall in the forest recently. I was marveling at the shower of colors autumn brings. I was thinking how the trees were nature's equivalent to fireworks. Each tree capturing sun light and directing it in bursts of color which hang in the sky only as long as they leaves hang on to their branches.

Last night's rain scrubbed the air clean of particulates and the sunlight streamed down unimpeded. It was brightly bounding in so many directions carrying so many degrees of color, it was mesmerizing. No camera, painting or any other artifice of engineering could capture such beauty.

I was on patrol, looking for a most loathsome foe and the autumn show was pleasuring my eyes so much I was, I am ashamed to admit, distracted. I should have been especially wary because the fallen leaves quilting the ground, created a patchwork of color that is natural camouflage for my most wary enemy.

I was at the edge of the woods at the far end of the back field. I got there by a circuitous route that carefully avoided the short path through the woods connecting to the main field where an attempt was made on my life earlier this summer.

In retrospect, I suppose it was the autumnal extravagance that altered my mood in such a way as to make me take a trail without remembering that one of the cardinal rules of guerilla warfare is that you never go where the enemy expects you to go.

A few yards down the trail I found the enemy's tracks. I knelt down to study them carefully. I could see there was no water in them and they were deep. He was near. Very near. Probably watching me at that very moment.

I knew I had to think fast but I was wrong. As it turns out I needed to think faster. Faster than I'd ever thought before.

I heard a rustle of the tree branches nearby then a large crack. I sprang backwards thrusting my legs against the stubborn earth with all my might. It wasn't enough. The soft ground absorbed most of my strength and I ended up flopping on my back not far from where I started with a horrifyingly clear view to what was to come.

An ash tree about ten meters high (33ft) with a thick trunk distinguished itself from the other ash trees surrounding it by moving in a straight line. Very much in the way that trees don't normally move. It was coming down. It was coming down on top of me.

Still not thinking fast enough, I had just enough time to register that several tons of tree was about to mash one couch potato and thereby create one hell of an interesting obituary when it made it's mad dash for the center of the earth.

I can tell you that when that heavy collection of baseball bats not yet born hit, it made a hell of a noise, which was magnified by the knowledge that I was about to die of course. The earth bounded away from me and the last memory I have of my doom was the sensation of being pummeled by about two hundred angry fists.

Darkness turned to light but I cannot say how long the process took. The light illuminating my eyelids beckoned me to open them. I did so slowly. I could see a blue hole in the colorized carpet of leaves in the tree tops above me.

A search of my immediate surroundings revealed that the trunk of the tree landed four centimeters (1 inch) from my heels and my position on the ground matched a space between the heavy branches perfectly. It was a group of smaller branches that had pummeled me.

Beaten, but not defeated, I decided to investigate what caused that tree, which nearly caused no one to be around to hear it fall in the forest, fall. I found my answer in short order. It was Spivey!

The stump had claw marks all over it and it was evident that the trunk had been gnawed through. However, it was gnawed in such a way as to cause the tree to fall onto the trail. The trail he knew I would some day take. Somehow, he'd guessed my move. He coupled that preternatural cunning with the super-sized patience he'd need to pull off the Herculean task of gnawing through all that tree.

As I stumbled back home to count my bruises it occurred to me that it was pure dumb luck that cancelled out my dumb stupidity. And if you want to compliment a fox tell him he's as clever as a turtle. It also occurred to me that perhaps the tree of the old question was an innocent victim. Perhaps the tree was hacked out of its prime years by a soulless, greedy, vindictive assassin looking to make a kill. Perhaps the truly nagging part of the question is that there is too much we don't know about the universe to answer it with confidence even if we pretend to have it with all our might.

Dr. Flubdubulous

Chapter Eight

Daily Star-Home and Leisure Section D-*October 16, 2004*

Of Bats and Men

Did you know that bats are mammals? It's true. In fact, they are the only flying mammals. Every time you see a bat flying you should say with pride, "There goes one of our boys!" Anything else you happen to see flying by without aluminum wings is a reptile. Or as I have come to see them, a relative of Spivey.

The ever changing vicissitudes of our climate and winding up on the wrong side of a meteorite, have forced reptiles to take smaller and more affectionate form but they retain the hatred of their kind for our kind in all its splendorous totality. Birds are the air force of the reptilian world and as such are the eyes and ears of their cohort.

Did you know that bats are becoming an endangered species? The Pennsylvania brown bat is going the way of the Do-Do. It's true. The smarty-pants know-it-alls will tell you that urban sprawl is mostly to blame. Construction crews routinely wake them up during the winter months which tends to kill them as awakened bats quickly use up their fat reserves. I think otherwise. I think the birds have been killing the bats.

So where's the outrage? Where's the letters of indignation when bats are being killed left and right? I've suffered a great deal of torment and insults because I've made the decision to fight back. Instead of praise, I receive invective.

Spivey doesn't care what anyone thinks and neither does his reptilian brethren. They only wish to kill every mammal they can. Absolutely none of which registers on the collective social consciousness. We've been taught bats are icky, rabies filled marauders that will suck your blood or throw themselves into bad, hairspray filled hairdos faster than you can say ewwww! We have also had it drilled into our heads that birds are noble symbols of freedom, love and peace which never do wrong.

Believe me you'll find lots more disease on one bird than any ten bats alive. And you won't find birds clearing the summer night air of blood sucking mosquitoes. Nor will you catch bats colluding to make war and bring death to their enemies (That is, unbeknownst to all but a few, the behavior of flying reptiles.)

Such facts come hard to the believers, the media zombies who forbid themselves to think. You know the ones I mean. We're in a bat holocaust and nary a sound comes from the Kiss the Pigeons Society. Yet, all parties feel they need to weigh in on my life and death struggle with Spivey.

Dr. Flubdubulous

From: Tom Anderson [mailto:Ufale@napkin.net]
Sent: Monday, October 17, 2004 6:34 AM
To: Dr. Flubdubulous
Subject: Cannibals gone mad

The Catholics now want to make Mother Teresa a saint? I think they are speeding up this traditionally slow process for a reason. The Catholics figure that since sainthood has always been a load of crap, why shouldn't we lower the bar like everyone else? Cher got an academy award, W became the leader of the free world, and a gangasta full of steroids is about to upstage baseball's saint. The complete disrespect for true merit has greatly enhanced my chances of receiving the Nobel Prize for Physics. Maybe you will win a Pulitzer, and Brandon will get a gold medal for figure skating. The looting of western civilization continues.

From: Dr. Flubdubulous [mailto:Dr.F@napkin.net]
Sent: Monday, October 17, 2004 8:34 AM
To: Tom Anderson
Subject: cannibals gone wild

Cher got an academy award for her portrayal of a slut who is confused about love. What else would you give an academy award to a woman for?

The Catholics have to shore up the South American take. They need a hero and beatification rules were made before T.V. Whatever the change, you can be assured your name won't be on the list.

When I do win the Pulitzer, I'll be sure to wrap it up and beat you to death with it.

Best,

PS What if you died and went to heaven and the first person you met there was Adolph Hitler? What if you find that he's there because God forgives all sins which kind of bothers you? God makes Hitler your roommate because you are having a hard time accepting that true grace is obtained through love and forgiving. What if after a while you start to like Hitler and, after many conversations with him, you start to feel that he was justified in many of the things he did on earth? What if just before you forgive Hitler you remember all the terrible things he did and you come to believe that you are not in heaven but in hell?! You find that the most effective method the devil has for spreading evil is to convince people that what they thought was evil isn't really evil after all. Every sin is only a rationale away from reality. What would you do then? I know what I'd do.

REDEMPTION

By Dr. Flubdubulous

PART 5

Falthor, Along the Frontier

Falthor stood still, occupying its place along the frontier as it had for uncounted centuries. There was not a hint of life on its bland ochre colored surface. The occasional crater left by an errant meteor were the only signs anything had ever occurred there.

Falthor should have been a coveted prize. It should have been used for a space station, a beacon, or used as an anchor for a great fleet but it wasn't any of those things. The unstable space of the frontier occasionally belched out gravimetric waves of such force the area was not desirable to anyone and thus no one even bothered to take the time to claim it. Mostly, it was left alone.

The shimmering contorted space of the Frontier cast an eerie glow onto the almost perfectly smooth face of Falthor. The contortions resulting from the periodic waves of gravity eventually reduced all protrusions on the surface.

A shadow was winding its way across the surface opposite the Frontier. The shadow was very small at first but then grew, vastly stretching in magnitude. It had a precise cross cut pattern and came to dominate most of the surface. The great Vicassian Armada had arrived.

SS Viper Command Ship of the first Imperial Fleet (IFF 1)

War Master Spivey was scrutinizing his paper map one last time when the com signal chimed. "Yes what is it?"

"We are almost on station sir," said a voice he did not recognize.

"I'll be there presently. Have the fleet form standard defensive position and send out scout ships and observation probes."

"Yes Sir,"

"Have Captain Hock report to the bridge."

"Yes Sir."

Spivey took one last glance at the map hoping faintly that something would jump out at him. He knew that his fleet had the advantage in numbers but then Harmon knew that too. It was all too easy. The defeat of the enemy lay in his weaknesses not in your strengths he reminded himself.

No matter he thought, even if the enemy's weaknesses were not apparent now they would be when they arrived. If they arrived. If that fat captain of the desks could be relied upon.

Spivey grabbed his side arm from its holster. He checked the power level to make sure it was at maximum. No Vicassian commander worth his victory stripes went into battle without a fully charged weapon, he thought. We'll see who will be slow to follow a command this day.

He took his personal lift to the bridge where he saw the bridge crew attending their scopes. They had the good sense not to look at him when he entered. Only Hock, as the Captain of record, could do that. Hock was standing by the large vidscreen dominating the front wall.

Hock turned and approached Spivey. He stopped a respectable distance and saluted.

"War Master, we have deployed the fleet as you ordered and sent out our scouts and probes."

"How goes things on Falthor?"

"Quiet as always, sir."

"I know that Hock, it's a rock in space," he said, his eyes narrowing. "I was referring to the gravimetric waves emanating from that damned Frontier."

Hock nodded slightly, "Yes Sir, there are no unusual readings so far."

"Have the Targ taken up their position on the far side of Falthor?"

"Yes sir, they await your orders."

"Let's hope they do."

Spivey stepped over to the tactical station and looked over the situation. Even getting a copy of the Kardon attack plan wasn't enough to ease his apprehension. He would have given it little credence had it not been for the second set of plans sent by real spies rather than the traitors in the office of the Star Commander.

Bold, confident Admiral Harmon was leading a fleet of traitors who'll turn away the minute the Armada shows its full self. I may go after his command ship myself, Spivey speculated. Just so long as the boy admiral is no more and the Armada continues to the Kardon home world for a victory the Emperor can savor-the old gas bag.

Spivey grunted at that last thought.

"Sir?" Hock said.

"Signal all captains of the Armada that Harmon is going to try his battering ram trick to knock us into the frontier. Tell them not to worry I have people on those ships, half the battle is already won."

Hock smiled at this latest bit of information. He knew Spivey had some form of treachery on tap. The War Master didn't succeed his every rival in the Empire as well as its enemies by playing fair.

Spivey lowered his voice a little, "Tell the Captains that they are forbidden to fire until I give the word."

"Yes, Sir."

Hock waited for more but Spivey stood looking at Falthor on the vidscreen. The curiosity got the better of Hock's judgment and he risked a question.

"Sir, do you want me to redeploy the fleet for the attack?"

Spivey turned his penetrating eyes at Hock, his red eyes seeming redder. But they were not lit with anger but rather, excitement. Hock could see that Spivey loved what was happening. He loved war. He would have nowhere to go if this

Armada was victorious and the war ended, Hock thought. But then, there's always another war.

"No, we know what he's going to do lets not let him know that."

"Yes sir."

Hock stepped over to the communications station to send the message. Spivey locked his hands behind his back and stared out at the vidscreen watching for any movement.

Command Ship Reach (C.S. 401k)

"Sir, the lead ship reports it encountered a probe and destroyed it," Prask announced from her comm station.

All activity on the bridge halted. All eyes were on the Admiral. He knew they were searching for his reaction. He smiled slowly.

"Excellent," was all he said.

"Yes, sir!" Prask said her voice loud enough for everyone to hear.

Zach walked over to the comm station casually. He leaned down to Prask and spoke in a low tone. "Send the final battle plans now. If you detect any subsequent communications I want to know about it right away. You understand?"

"Yes sir," she said her hands already dancing across the numerous buttons and touch pads on her console.

SS Viper Command Ship of the first Imperial Fleet (IFF 1)

"Sir, one of our probes has just been destroyed," an ensign almost shouted from his comm station to Captain Hock.

"Did it send any information before it was destroyed?" Hock asked.

"It's destruction was the message," Spivey said levelly.

"Yes sir," Hock replied.

Spivey turned to the young ensign, "What sector was the probe in?"

"The sixth sir."

"Hmmh, straight at us."

"As you predicted sir," Hock said.

"Yes," Spivey said and looked down at the gray plastisteel deck plates for a moment. "He wants to end this in a final blazing battle."

"It would seem so sir,"

A look of contempt swept over Spivey's face. "Yes it would," he spat out. Turning to the ensign he said, "Inform the Targ commander our quarry has been sighted. Tell him to remain on station behind the planetoid until we signal him to advance."

Hock immediately recognized the danger in what the War Master was planning. Splitting his forces was giving an opportunity to the enemy and Harmon was not the sort to overlook opportunity. Hock, though he was risking immediate execution by doing so, said, "Sir?"

To Hock's relief Spivey did something he almost never did. He grinned. The feared War Master looked almost giddy. Somehow he'd gleaned something from the information that Hock had not.

"Don't you see it Hock? He's going to form up for a battering ram."

"Sir, if he does use his battering ram technique won't we need the fire power of the Targ to stop him?"

"He's confident but he's no fool. He's under orders not to risk losing his fleet. We must make him think the advantage lies with him so he'll press his attack. We'll let him push us back to the frontier then we'll seal his fate with the Targ. The frontier will hold him in place while we drop a Chunny tree on him."

Spivey waited a second for his words to sink into Hock's brain and when he saw the expression of confusion on Hock's face change to one of understanding, Spivey smiled. Neither Hock, nor anyone else on the bridge had ever seen Spivey smile.

Spivey turned back to the young ensign still standing at the comm station who was now smiling too. "Ensign, tell the Targ commander to monitor our telemetry and keep Falthor between his fleet and the enemy." Turning back to Hock he said, "I wouldn't want to spring the trap too early. I don't want a single enemy ship to escape destruction this day."

Hock nodded feeling more confident than he'd been since they'd left the home world for this battle.

Fighting Ship Valiant (F.S. 2308)

"Captain, the coordinates have been loaded into the navicomputer and the count-down to launch of the battle sequence has begun. I've taken the comm station offline as per the Admiral's orders"

Julie looked up at the young lieutenant. He was tall, young, ambitious and not part of the co-conspirators of her senior staff. It was his first voyage on the *Valiant*. She needed to get him off the bridge to make the necessary adjustments to the navicomputer.

It would seem, even though her information on the overall battle plan was less than one piece, her officers were correct about the Admiral's intentions. He was going to sacrifice himself in this battle. Why else would he put himself at the head of the battering ram in a command ship? Command Ships were lightly armed and not very heavily shielded. They were built for speed mostly.

She hated the thought of disobeying orders on her first tour as captain of a capital ship but what choice did she have? The Admiral was more important to the cause than ten capital ships even if he didn't know it. If his tin plated command ship was destroyed at any point in the coming battle, the remaining fighting ships would break off and make a run for it. He had to know this and yet he was risking it all on a show of bravado that would restore loyalty to the mutinous crews of the fleet.

The true curiosity was the order to shut off communications. The obvious reason was to prevent turncoat ships from coordinating their efforts but the admiral never did anything for obvious reasons. Still, the black out would work to her advantage. When she did break with the plan, no one could contact her to tell her otherwise. Perhaps she could say she misunderstood her orders at the court martial. No, in the end, she knew she'd have to take the responsibility herself.

"Thank you lieutenant, you are relieved," she said casually and turned to her hand held vidscreen.

"Sir?"

She looked up, "I said you are relieved."

"Sir, regulations state that in battle the-"

"Yes, the bridge must have a full compliment. I am aware of the regulations they were explained to me when I was made captain."

She let that bit of sarcasm bite into his pride while she held his eyes in her stare.

"Sir, it's just that . . . I . . Uh"

"It's all right lieutenant," she said changing her hard stare to a more congenial expression, letting him off the hook. "We won't need navigation or communications. Our senior officers can handle the bridge, I want every spare hand on fire suppression. This is going to be a rough one and I want the ship in top shape for our victory celebrations."

The young lieutenant smiled, "Yes sir," he barked and headed for the lift doors.

She could see Pleat was already headed for the navicomputer as the doors slid closed behind the young lieutenant.

Command Ship Reach (C.S. 401k)

"Are the ships forming up?" Zach asked Plex.

Plex startled at the admirals voice. He'd been concentrating so hard on what the vidscreens were telling him about the coming battle that he didn't hear the usual cry of "Admiral on the bridge!" much less Zach's footsteps as he strode over to him.

"Easy Plex, the battle didn't start yet."

Plex smiled, "Yes sir. Our fleet is forming up as per your orders now. Our long range scanners have detected the enemy fleet dead ahead. But . . ."

"But what?"

"The Targ do not appear to be with them. We think they may be hiding behind Falthor itself but it is more likely the alliance has fallen apart.

"They are there believe it."

"But, why would they split their forces when they'll need their combined fire power to defend against our mutual-offense formation?"

"He wants to lure me in close to the gravity waves emanating from the frontier. He figures they will serve to separate our ships and thereby reduce our offensive capability. The Targ will show themselves when it is time to hammer us to the wall of the Frontier."

Plex was amazed at this analysis. It was clever and cogent but was any of it real? There seemed to be a great deal based on variables whose outcome couldn't possibly be calculated. And yet, Zach seemed to have done so, to his own satisfaction anyway.

Plex leaned in toward Zach so that the prebattle noises of the busy bridge would cover his voice. "Zach, what the hell is this plan of yours?"

"Plex, you're about to find out."

Zach stepped to the front of the brightly lighted bridge. "Attention!" he said in a voice he hadn't used since his academy days. Everyone snapped to attention instantly, Plex included.

Falthor, Along the Frontier

The many ships of the Vicassian fleet parked near the space side of Falthor began to move. They spread out to form a wall of ships several dozen deep. The wall started forward toward the tiny lights of distant stars.

One of the tiny lights seemed to be growing in size. The dot increasing in size and detail as the Vicassian fleet lumbered toward it. It wasn't long before bits of blue light began to travel between the two respective fleets. The Vicassian fleet stopped its forward momentum.

One by one the ships of the Vicassian fleet broke off their attack and started streaking back towards Falthor. The Kardon fleet clustered as one massive entity in close pursuit.

SS Viper Command Ship of the first Imperial Fleet (IFF 1)

"War Master, our ships report mostly minor damage and are withdrawing to the first marker. The Yewl has not reported in. One of our scout ships reports that the Yewl was heavily damaged while laying Guwaba mines on the enemy's enhanced shield net."

"Excellent,"

"Orders sir?"

"Yes, tell all commanders to form an Alpha defense at the first marker."

Hock stepped closer to Spivey when the young comm ensign hurried off to carry out his orders. The atmosphere was electric. Even though they were technically in retreat, spirits were soaring. The dreaded boy admiral didn't hit them with any surprises. He hadn't done anymore than scorch a few hull plates and he seemed to be falling into the trap.

Even Spivey himself looked to be in a rare good mood. Hock did not ask but then he was sure he didn't have to. The old war master had a tendency to express his thoughts during battle.

"That's it Hock. He's committed himself and we haven't sustained near the losses projected. We're going to give him a grand reception at the first marker."

"Yes sir," Hock said, with an enthusiasm that didn't quite match what he was really thinking. This was all too easy. Maybe our ships broke off too soon. Maybe their new weapons weren't as effective as previously thought. You can't wrestle a Teela Cat and not get scratched.

"I can read your mind Hock," Spivey said. "Don't worry, he may be toying with us but he hasn't seen all our cards yet."

Playing off the heightened mood of his men, Spivey called to the comm officer loud enough for all on the bridge to hear, "Ensign, send my message to our friends in the Kardon fleet."

"Yes sir!" the ensign replied without looking away from his console.

"You see Hock? We can have more than the Targ for allies."

Hock said nothing but watched the vidscreen intently. Several ships from the rear of the great battering ram formation peeled off and reversed course. Then several more. The bridge crew let out a cheer when a huge quantity separated itself from the main body and then dispersed. Less than half the fleet was left when it finally got back into formation.

Incredibly, the Kardon fleet kept coming. The Admiral was not backing down. He was Hock thought, even with the best of luck, on a suicide mission. He has to know that. Perhaps his pride will not let him avoid a battle he's already lost. Perhaps it's arrogance. This was a great man. Indeed, one deserving of a poem.

"He sacrifices himself now. Perhaps you will write one of your poems about him when your back at your desk eh Hock?"

Hock said nothing. The admiral deserved better than to be discussed with the gloating Spivey. They both watched as the Vicassian Armada reached the first marker and began forming up. They then watched as the space between the two sides grew smaller.

Command Ship Reach (C.S. 401k)

"How many left the formation?"

"The exact number you ordered to, Admiral."

"Excellent," Zach said and walked to the scanning station. "Any losses reported?" he asked the Lieutenant Commander studying his screens.

"No confirmed losses sir, but the *Valiant* does not seem to be on station."

Zach considered this for a moment. It wouldn't seriously affect his plans if the *Valiant* was lost and he was certain its officers and crew wouldn't trade sides.

"Pleat!"

"Sir?" Pleat said, already at his side.

"Pleat, go down to long range scanning and see if you can locate the *Valiant*, she's not on station."

"Yes sir."

Zach waited three seconds after the doors to the bridge closed behind Pleat to motion to Plex who was at the front of the bridge.

Plex came over immediately. "Sir."

"Plex what do you know of my replacement on the *Valiant*?"

"Captain Bedford, she was hand picked by the Star Commander himself. She comes from a good family, has a good

190

record and is considered by many to be a competent commander."

Zach said nothing, thought about it for a second then sat in the command chair. Plex knew that Zach almost never sat in the command chair and certainly not during a battle. It was his habit to circulate to the various command stations. He always kept at least one eye on the front vidscreen at all times. Plex's Suh-vak senses told him there was something more to the question.

"Why?"

"The *Valiant* isn't on station."

"We can't stop for it now."

"Yes, I am aware that I must leave them to their fate but perhaps we may be able to nudge fate a little."

"You want me to-"

"Sir!" the Lieutenant Commander at the scanner station called out. "The Vicassians have set up what appears to be a defensive formation just past Falthor."

Zach turned back to Plex, "I have Pleat checking on them now. Let's attend to the good War Master."

Zach tripped the life support failure switch on the command chair armrest console signaling all hands to don their encounter suits. Every hand on the Reach was in their suits in less than sixty seconds.

Zach knew that each and every member of his crew was dying to know why he'd put them all in hot bulky encounter suits when they hadn't really had a hull breach or failure in the life support systems. He also knew that he wouldn't have time to explain it.

"Helm head straight for the center of the Vicassian formation. And redirect all shield power to our front."

Fighting Ship Valiant (F.S. 2308)

It wasn't hard to find the Admiral's Command ship among the massive fleet. He was characteristically up front. His was the lead ship. But command ships were designed more for watching battles rather than actually fighting in them. Putting the

Reach at the very tip of his battering ram was reckless in the extreme, Julie thought.

The *Valiant's* officers were right to be concerned. Whatever the Admiral's overall strategy was, a little help from the Valiant's bulk and fire power wouldn't hurt. After all the non-conspirators were shooed from the bridge it was small matter for the *Valiant's* senior officers to tuck her in just below the wash of the *Reach's* massive starboard engine.

They would have to stay close but not too close.

SS Viper Command Ship of the first Imperial Fleet (IFF 1)

"Sir, more of the Kardon fleet is breaking off its attack."

"How many remain?" Hock asked the crewman at the scanner station.

"Five ships, sir."

"Five," Hock said under his breath. That couldn't be right. The first engagement was hardly anything. Now they were to be treated to victory without effort. This was too easy.

"Hock, why so worried, you'll earn your victory stripes today," Spivey said. "We're going after the lead ship ourselves."

Hock turned quickly at the sound of Spivey's voice. He'd been concentrating on the conundrum so hard he'd almost forgotten Spivey was still on the bridge.

"Sir, I advise caution."

"Yes, of course you do."

"Sir, the enemy will be within weapons range in one minute," the helmsman reported.

"Excellent, put us in front of that lead ship and prepare to fire all guns."

Hock turned to the central vidscreen. There wasn't much more he could do at this point. The decision had been made. He only hoped that the decision was the right one.

Hock could see the sleek white ship leading the others. Only one was made for battle, the rest were lightly armed and built more for speed than anything. Next to them, the fighting ship looked like a lumbering mine ship.

"They're firing sir," someone called out behind him. Hock didn't move. He didn't reach for anything to hold onto. He was still a captain even if there was a War Master aboard.

Hock could see the Lancet Torpedoes fired from all ships except the fighting ship, streaking toward them. They left a red streaks of light behind them. It was a futile gesture. It was merely a snarl, or perhaps the shaking of a fist but it posed no threat. The fleet was too vast for so small a number of torpedoes to do any significant damage.

At the last instant all the torpedoes swerved to converge at one point just outside shield range. The explosion was blinding. It sent a shock wave of incredible intensity that literally shoved back the ships of the mighty armada and created a hole in the wall of ships for the attacking ships to burst through.

Hock picked himself up off the floor and dashed for the scanning station when he saw the main vidscreen was out. He got there just in time to see the Admiral and his ships pulling away from the Armada towards the frontier. Several ships of the Armada were already in pursuit.

"So your admiral had one surprise after all," Spivey spat at Hock. He turned to the comm officer, "Have the Targ cut him off. I want all ships in pursuit of those ships. Now!"

Command Ship Reach (C.S. 401)

"We're through Admiral, and they're coming after us."

"Has anyone fired on us yet?"

"No sir, they are not in weapons range yet?"

"Good, turn off all shields, lights, and life support and route all power to the engines."

"Yes sir,"

The lights went out on the bridge. It was dark except for the main vidscreen and the various lights on the touch pads and consoles. It was strange, Plex thought, attacking with a command ship and wearing encounter suits during battle like they did in the days of his grandfather.

"Now what?" asked Plex.

"Now we see if I'm as clever a planner as everyone seems to think."

"Sir, there is an unidentified ship to starboard," the young officer at the scanner station said.

"How close?"

"Two thousand standard lengths."

Zach and Plex exchanged puzzled looks.

"Can't be one of theirs," Zach said.

"No, couldn't be," Plex agreed.

"Sir, what do you want me to do?"

"Maintain course and heading, we cannot change the plan now," Zach said as he started for the doors at the rear of the bridge.

"Where are you going?" Plex asked.

"I'm going to look out the window and see who's off our starboard quarter."

As he got to the doors they slipped open and Pleat was there. Zach stopped short.

"Sir, the ship off our starboard quarter is the *Valiant*."

"The *Valiant*!? That's not their duty station." He turned and headed over to the scanning station. "How far behind us is the enemy?"

"About two minutes but since we routed all power to the engines they've not been able to catch up. The *Valiant* is falling behind. They'll make contact in one minute."

Zach thought about it. The battle plans couldn't be altered. There was nothing he could do for the *Valiant*.

"Maintain course and speed."

"You're not going back for them?" Plex blurted out.

"Ah, sir-" Pleat began.

"I can't go back for them. I know that our friends are on the *Valiant*." He turned to Pleat, "I know your son is on the *Valiant*. But, I cannot alter the plan, the battle is not yet won."

"Sir, we just picked up the Targ on our screens. They're moving to cut us off.," the helmsman reported.

Zach looked at Plex and Pleat. "Maintain course and heading."

Fighting Ship Valiant (F.S. 2308)

A tremor raced through the ship and Julie felt it through the dampeners in her command chair. She knew it was the first shots from their pursuers. They were testing her shields' strengths and weaknesses.

"Weapons"

"Yes, Sir,"

"After the next barrage by our friends, release a count of Beggar mines. But don't fire them off, just release them."

"Yes Sir"

At this speed they wouldn't take long to reach their destination. Another tremor, slightly more intense made its way to Julie's chair. She nodded to the weapons officer.

"Explosions sir, the lead ship following us is out of action."

A cheer rose up from the bridge crew. She was about to remind them that they were facing long odds but then thought better of it. Let them have their moment she thought, there were not many left.

"Reduce power and prepare to come about."

"Sir, the Targ just appeared on our screens. They're heading for the Admiral's ship."

"Belay that last order. Put us between the Admiral and the Targ."

SS Viper Command Ship of the first Imperial Fleet (IFF 1)

Hock could see the lead elements of the Armada exchanging weapons fire with the lone Fighting Ship. Harmon was not known for leaving any of his men during battle but he'd left the *Valiant* to certain annihilation. There was no way a lone ship wedged between the Targ and the Armada could survive.

The little zips of blue light began to increase in intensity. The *Valiant* was putting up a good fight but it was hopeless. Hock hoped it would go quickly for them.

A flash of light erupted at the head of he formation pursuing the old Fighting Ship. When the flash was over Hock could see the lead ship was out of action and the two ships on either side of it were badly damaged. A smart move by the commander of the Fighting Ship but a delaying tactic only. The ships following the pursuers began filtering around the damaged vessels on their way to destroy the *Valiant*.

What was that ship doing there? Perhaps they were the only crew left still loyal to the Admiral. Soon they would die with him. A gesture perhaps?

"The Targ are advancing sir. Shall I have them open fire?" a voice behind him asked. Hock wasn't sure if the question was directed at him or the great War Master but he didn't much care. This glorious fight had become a Teeper hunt. Soon, when the Targ were on station and the hunted ships were wedged up against the frontier, they would be slaughtered like a farm animal.

"Tell the Targ commander he is welcome to *try* and get our quarry before us," Spivey said then chuckled.

Hock strained to see the Admiral's command ship but it was a distant speck. Somehow the admiral had been able to keep ahead of them but ahead of him was the Frontier. At these speeds it was as good as a solid wall.

Hock went over to the scanning station to get a view of the overall battle as it was unfolding. It would be easier to watch it conclude from there.

Command Ship Reach (C.S. 401)

"All stop!" Zach said louder than he wanted to. He could feel Pleat behind him and he heard Plex breathing heavy in his encounter suit, straining to not ask why he was stopping the ship now when the *Valiant* was probably already destroyed.

"Shut down everything except the engines and helm control. Signal our escorts to keep moving." He could hear all of their thoughts. They were wondering if he'd gone nuts. Lights began snapping off at all stations. At least they're still following orders no matter how bizarre he thought.

"Sir?"

It was Pleat. Zach didn't want to talk just now. With two enemy fleets bearing down on him, the frontier looming in front of him and the ship essentially blinded by his last command, this was not a time for discussion. His timing couldn't afford to be a second off.

He reminded himself that Pleat had a son on that ship. It took all his will to turn around even though he had no real reason to face the screens since he'd had them shut down.

"Yes Pleat, I know," he said and smiled slightly. "I know this is confusing. Whatever the *Valiant* did, it slowed down the Vicassians. I need them closer for the final part of my plan. We are not going back for the them. I'm sorry."

"Yes sir" Pleat said without expression.

Fighting Ship Valiant (F.S. 2308)

"Captain, the *Reach* has come to a dead stop!"

"How far are the Targ from him?"

"We will be between them in one minute."

That wasn't the question she'd asked but it was the answer she'd wanted. The question she couldn't ask was, what would they do when they got there? A frontal assault by one ship on an entire fleet wouldn't buy the Admiral much time.

"Put us parallel to the *Reach* with our starboard side to the Targ."

"Yes, Captain!" the helmsman yelled over the noise of the already reversing engines.

Command Ship Reach (C.S. 401k)

The bridge was dark and quiet except for swishing of the breathers on the encounter suits. Frost was forming on some of the consoles. Although Zach couldn't feel it through his suit, he knew the atmosphere on the bridge was becoming frigid.

"Turn on the scanners."

The scanners popped to life and showed the Vicassians where he wanted them. But the Targ were much closer than he wanted them. The *Valiant's* efforts to save him may have just destroyed him. He would still achieve victory but neither he nor anyone else on the *Reach* was going to be at the victory celebration.

The Targ had already launched a startling number of antimatter missiles at the *Reach*. Even with all power to the shields they probably wouldn't hold.

"Prepare . . ."

"Sir!"

"I see it."

Zach saw the *Valiant* zip into position between him and the missiles. The *Valiant* absorbed nearly all of them. They exploded with a brilliant blue green flash.

"This is it! Full speed ahead. Reroute all shield power to the front shields."

Fighting Ship Valiant (F.S. 2308)

Julie felt the missiles drive into her ship. The command chair leaped upward and sent her sprawling on the deck. A dozen claxon's came to life while smoke filled the bridge. She started to get up again and the ship shook violently as several more missiles hit the starboard side.

The bridge had become a swirling vortex of smoke, sound and flashing lights. Wounded crew members howled in pain, a jumble of voices came from the comm stations and the acrid smell of burning electronics was suffocating.

Julie got to her feet and felt heavier. "Status!" she yelled over the din.

Someone called out, "Captain, all systems are down."

It was Pleat, and the expression on his normally expressionless face told her all she needed to know. She stepped over several prostrate crew members in various states of dying to get to one of the last working scanner stations. She saw the rear end of the *Reach* heading for the Frontier at explosive speed. At least, the Admiral made his escape, she thought. An escape made courtesy of the lives of his former crew and a once great Fighting Ship.

The ship shuttered slightly and she knew exactly what that meant. The Targ had closed in for the kill. They were cutting her ship apart with laser beams. Savoring the moment and conserving their missiles. It wouldn't be long now. Perhaps she could slow them down by maneuvering in amongst them.

She started to move but felt heavier, as if someone turned up the gravity on the bridge. "Pleat we have to get this ship moving again."

Pleat looked up from his station and said, "We are moving Captain."

"What!?"

"Gravity waves emanating from the Frontier are pulling us in."

The shuddering stopped. The Targ were getting into a better position before finishing them off. They didn't want to be sucked into the Frontier anymore than she did. She slapped at the all-call touch pad on the console, "Attention all crew, This is the Captain, abandon ship, abandon ship! I say again, everyone to the life pods, abandon ship!"

She turned from the scanner console to see who she could help off the ship. The main vidscreen was working again. On it was the shrinking image of the *Reach* heading for the Frontier. She could hear explosions throughout the ship as bulkheads collapsed. "Pleat!" she yelled just before everything went dark.

Chapter Nine

From: Dolly Anderson [mailto:kittygrl@napkin.net]
Sent: Wednesday, October 19, 2004 4:10 PM
To: Sue Green
Subject: Baby Shower

I'm sorry but I can't make your daughter's baby shower. Andy has decided to build a "perimeter fence." He's using heavy field stone and I'm worried he might hurt himself in an accident. How he could enclose our entire property is a mystery to me but he is determined. I'll let you know.

Dolly,

PS I'll send my gifts to the house.

Original Message Deleted for Reasons Unknown

From: Dr. Flubdubulous [mailto:DrF@napkin.net]
Sent: Wednesday, October 19, 2004 7:10 PM
To: Tom Anderson

Subject: Re: Perimeter Fence

To answer your questions: Yes, I am building a
barrier fence. And yes, I may never finish it
given the size of my property but every foot of
wall is one less foot the enemy has to maneuver
with. Every yard of wall reduces his options
by just that much. This is a war wherein
victory rides as much on our will as it does on
bombs, bullets, and bayonets.
Best,

PS To answer your other question, Yes I will

meet with you however, if you recall, you were

to tell me when you'd be available and you

never got back to me. You let me know, and

I'll be there but now, I gotta get back to my

victory wall.

Daily Star-Home and Leisure Section D-*October 30, 2004*

Death Time

Sometimes I play a game in my head wherein I rank
people based on my desire to have lunch with them. In my
opinion, a relaxing lunch is just about the best way one can spend
time with another. Just being famous, or being rich, or being rich
and famous, does not automatically get you on the short list. At
the same time, being an insurance salesman, guidance counselor
or producer won't automatically exclude you.

A close friend of mine, a man always high on the list,
passed away recently. He was bright, articulate, an expert in his

field, funny, friendly and above all, genuine. He will be missed until of course, all those who miss him are themselves gone.

I spend a great deal of time contemplating death. It's inevitable you know. Whole galaxies and even our universe will die. Everything dies.

Einstein wrote that time space and matter are connected in a very fundamental way and I would add that time and death are related. Time finishes off all life eventually.

What if most life in this galaxy operated at a different level? I mean you're conscious right? But we know that your consciousness really only exists because of a multitude of chemical reactions taking place at the atomic and sub-atomic level. And those reactions are taking place at a speed which seems phenomenally fast to us. So it could be argued that that is really where life is. It's as if our consciousness is just a byproduct of the real show. Like a parasite living on the skin of a whale thinking that the whale is not the key player in the relationship.

More likely we didn't know what to look for. Perspective is important. Different sizes have different time scale dynamics.

I have no doubt my friend knew he was mortal. I'm certain he spent most of his life ignoring that fact, as most of us do. Yet, his life had worth. He enriched the lives of those around him. He gave without reserve.

Perhaps the best we can hope for is to cheat time out of relishing its victory over us. The only way to do that is the way my friend did. By making the lives of those around us full of life.

Time's mission is to erase meaning. The more meaning we can preserve the less time matters.

You can spend your life marking time with the acquisition of material wealth and power. You may relegate family interaction to the holidays. You may work your way past the best moments filled with untapped potential. However, someday, one hundred trillion years from now, the last star in our universe will burn out. Then where will you be? Huh?

Diabetametrics: The Unreal Story of a True Superhero

Chapter 6

Howard decided to cash in his silver dollars. His decision was not based on a demand by his reduced circumstances but rather he was motivated by a desire to rid himself o his former life. The one he was no longer permitted to live. For some reason he wasn't interested in any of it anymore.

What Howard wanted was to go back to when the girls were young. When his life was less complicated. When he was a hero, a superhero.

He left the house with his bag of one hundred or so silver dollars in an old camp Merrydale bag, also a remnant from his childhood. The bag was a simple hunter green nylon sack with a rubberized inside liner and a draw string. The day camp, like his childhood, was long gone but the bag looked brand new. The white letters in the round logo were as crisp and easy to read as they were the day he received it.

Howard stepped off the stoop and swung the bag over his shoulder. The day was cold, gray, and still. He estimated the temperature had dropped ten degrees since yesterday. The ice on the walk crunched under his feet and he leaned into his stride magnifying the noise as much as he could.

He headed up the deserted street toward Carlton Avenue. A white sheen of frost, refusing to give way to the sun, clung to nearly every surface. There were sparkles everywhere.

The coins had been painstakingly collected by Howard in his preteen years. He kept them in cardboard holders wrapped in plastic. He'd kept them in pristine condition for the day he would give them to his son. Now all bets were off. The girls were the only sons he had and they were not interested in the coin collection.

He made the left onto Carlton heading up towards Main Street. The cold air from the wind sweeping down Carlton stabbed at his exposed skin. He didn't care.

Despite the cold his thoughts brought him away. He usually reflected on many things but today the memories came in a jumble. Faces, places, smells passed the window of his mind just slow enough for recognition and then they were gone. Nothing he could grab on to.

It seemed to him that he'd gotten to the railroad underpass in record time. That is, he couldn't remember what had happened from when he turned on to Carlton to that point.

Going up the slight incline after the bridge reminded him of the hefty cargo slung over his shoulder. He shifted the bag to his other shoulder. He took a moment to consider his present state.

The feeling was not quite insane but it definitely wasn't sane. It wasn't an out of body experience but it was close. It was a foggy sensation of calmly peace. He was there but not *of* the situation. If a fire broke out he might just sit and watch it rather than run for his life. Sometimes it was a pleasant sensation but mostly it was disconcerting. He was himself but only three quarters so.

It was certainly better than the other states of being he cycled through in the course of a day. The worst was when he was crashing. His entire body went into extreme rebellion and refused to stop sending sick messages until he fed it some sort of sugar. Next there was the angry phase. While in it, he became angry about everything. More disconcerting than the angry phase was what he called the giddy phase. There he laughed and delighted over the most inane and unfunny things.

His emotions/feelings, his state of being, was a runaway train unleashed by molecules he couldn't see. Chemicals he couldn't control. An unseen enemy that struck at will and forced him to alter his tactics accordingly. It was a war fought daily with no indication of who won the day in the end.

Through all these phases there was an underlying feeling of exhaustion which Howard was not sure he came to have from the terrorist molecules tearing around his system or was a natural consequence of his situation. He did know that every time he thought about it, he became depressed and anxious.

He'd built up walls to protect himself from the concept of his mortality. He'd worked hard at making all the infirm parts of his life firm. He'd endeavored to believe all the lies people usually construct between themselves and the harsh realities of a harsh universe.

His thoughts were interrupted by his arrival at the corner of Carlton and Main. He had to remind himself which way was the proper way to the bank. He looked both ways then turned left, shifted the money to his other shoulder, and started crunching towards the bank with a purposeful stride.

When he got to the bank he paused to collect his thoughts. He scanned main street and the large parking lot of the food store across the street. Not much was happening. The cold kept those who were not at work or school in their homes. He turned to his left and made his way up the long walk to the lobby entrance and stepped inside.

The bank was its usual self. Mrs. Bowersox was behind the long counter which ran along the wall opposite the door. There were three people already waiting in the long serpentine corridor of red velvet ropes which dominated the main room.

Howard walked to his proper place in line. He did not anticipate a long wait and kept his specie filled Camp Merrydale bag on his shoulder. He heard the door behind him open but he did not turn to see who'd come in. He thought he heard the sound of running feet.

"Nobody move!" someone from behind him yelled.

Despite the order, Howard turned toward the voice as did every pair of eyes in the bank. They all saw a short man at the main door holding a sawed-off shotgun. He was wearing a thick down jacket, a ski mask, gloves and a pair of light weight running shoes. If this were a movie, Howard thought, the man with the shotgun would be the one to yell "Nobody move."

The man at the door's two compatriots ran to opposite ends of the large room that served as the bank's main business area. One of the men flew over the counter and slapped Mrs. Bowersox in the face knocking her to the floor.

"Otta my way bitch!" he shouted.

The man behind the counter started to empty the cash drawers into a sack. The whole scene was such a compilation of movie clichés that Howard would not have been one bit surprised had a director suddenly yelled cut because someone forgot to scream when poor old Mrs. Bowersox got slapped.

Howard thought about it some more and determined that it was all really happening. These thugs were robbing and brutalizing these people. The more he thought about it the angrier he got. All the fear and self loathing came bubbling and roiling out of the deepest recesses of his mind, the parts he'd systematically cut off. They hit his psyche like super heated steam.

Howard's fear of death, fear of loss, fear of fear, all hit a single point all at once. It was too much for him. The man with the shotgun became the manifestation of all his fear and grief and anger over the past year.

He moved without thinking. He slipped the Merrydale bag off his shoulder as he spun counter clockwise. By the time he'd made it half way through his revolution, the cord was fully extended and the bag laden with heavy coins was moving at top speed. It hit the gunman with every ounce of Howard's stockpiled rage on the right side of his head killing him instantly.

The gunman's body convulsed just as the bag did its worst. The shotgun went off. Three pellets caught Howard in his left thigh. The force knocked Howard down which saved his life because while the man behind the counter was occupied and did not see what was happening, the other gun wielding thug did and he tried to shoot Howard. The bullet passed directly through the space Howard's head had occupied an instant before.

Howard reached for the shotgun. He yanked it out of the dead man's hand and cycled the pump ejecting the spent shell, chambering a new one as he pointed it at the man who'd nearly just shot him and was preparing to try again. They fired at the same time. The shotgun blast hit the man in the exact center of his chest. His torso splattered on the wall behind him and dripped down in long red streaks. The man dropped straight down and flopped on the floor.

His bullet, the last one he would ever fire, lodged in the receiver of the shotgun Howard had used to kill him with. The shotgun was knocked out of Howard's hands and clattered on the blood covered tile floor.

The man behind the counter who had dove for cover when the second round of shooting started, poked his head above the counter. He saw Howard stagger to his feet with blood streaming from his left leg and the broken shotgun lying on the floor. He eyes locked with Howard's and he smiled broadly as he raised his gun, confident that he held the high ground.

Howard reached down and snatched his Camp Merrydale bag in one hand and hurled it at the thug as he charged the counter. This maneuver so shocked and unnerved the gunman that he didn't move at first allowing Howard to close the distance. Some part of Howard's profile getting larger as he approached stirred a sense of self preservation and the gunman took a step back as he started shooting wildly.

As Howard dove over the counter a bullet crashed through his chest and tore out the lower half of his left lung. He came down on top of his killer. The young thug was flattened by the force.

Howard though grievously wounded was still enraged. He'd been robbed of so much this past year. He'd been a victim for so long. He'd had to take and take and take. Now he determined that he was going to give it. This punk was going to take it.

Howard grabbed an oversized stapler that had landed on the floor. He struck the thug in the forehead. The man grunted as his head was thrown back. Howard hit him again before he could recover. He hit him over and over and continued even after there was a sickening crack as the thug's skull was broken.

Howard, drenched in blood, breathing heavy, finally ceased his attack. He got off the prostrate thug. He sat back leaning against the counter. He felt light headed and a little cold. There were noises and light. It was cold, very cold. Then there was a man in a paramedic uniform leaning over him.

"Sir, can you hear me?"

"Yes," Howard croaked.

"What's your name?"

"Huh?"

The paramedic checked Howard's pulse. "Who are you sir? We're gonna do everything we can to help. You're gonna be fine. You're a hero."

"I was a hero once" Howard said, then died.

From: Tom Anderson [mailto:Ufale@napkin.com]
Sent: Sunday, February 18, 2004 9:09 PM
To: Dr. Flubdubulous
Subject: Ah Youth!

A long time ago, I enjoyed a cold slurpee on
the hot sidewalk of an Islip 7-11. It was
bliss. A high standard set at a young age. No
experience in my overindulged adulthood can
compete with the novel pleasures of my
underprivileged childhood.

Tom

PS I'll have to get back to you on our meeting
because I'm going on a trip to Vermont. BUT !! As
soon as I get back we have to meet! I am not
comfortable concerning this thing with the turtle
you call Spivey.

From: Dr. Flubdubulous [mailto:DrF@napkin.com]
Sent: Sunday, October 31, 2004 10:29 PM
To: Tom Anderson
Subject: Re: Ah Youth!

I agree those were better days. It was before
the disillusionment of adulthood, before
Reaganism, before anyone questioned the concept
of the Mammoth Car, before I got a severe ass
kicking by Father Time and before the
excitement of possibility left for parts
unknown. Now the food is dangerous, the four
walls are safe and all the deadly animals have
left their cages and roam the zoo in the
twilight. Maybe it is best that one cannot

208

live in the past because were it possible, I
would spend all my time there.

Best,

PS The 7-11 episode does stand out in my mind
as the one of the very few instances we didn't
buy beer. Weird!

PPS Enjoy your trip to Vermont. Hey, if by
chance you come across any overpaid, under
worked, narcissistic, disconnected, amoral
dilatants while your on your weeklong, larger
than life spendfeast, tell them that I and all
the other "boors" who are bathed in their
contempt while we labor to make their vacations
possible, say hi.

To: Executive Director Stone, Evangelical

Hospital

     I have decided a boycott of your Hospital

to protest the discrimination I've encountered

in my attempts to achieve employment as a

brain surgeon. Despite having repeatedly

explained my credientials and skills (see

below) I've never been granted so much as an

interview let alone a full time position. Wich

I deserve.

Sincerely,

Dr. Flubdubulous

<u>Skills and Credentials</u>

-Ability to clean hands real good.

-Good time keeping skills

-Red two books on brainology

-Good with people

-Excellent cleaning skills

-G.E.D. Diploma

REDEMPTION

By Dr. Flubdubulous

PART 6

SS Viper Command Ship of the first Imperial Fleet (IFF 1)

Spivey watched as what was left of the *Valiant* was being pulled into the Frontier. They sacrificed their lives for the boy Admiral who led them to ruin he concluded. Some of the escape pods had made it past the gravity waves but most were going to that infernal part of space forever.

The only thing standing between him and total victory, he thought, was the Admiral's ship itself. He had to see it destroyed. Nothing would please the Emperor more and a happy Emperor is a good thing indeed.

The Admiral's command ship was heading away at top speed but he had no where to go. The Frontier would see to that.

"Sir."

"Yes Hock what is it?"

"Shall we send out emergency ships for the crew of that Fighting Ship?"

"The battle is not over Hock. I want every ship to pursue the *Reach*. Do you understand? I want every molecule of that ship and it's commander blown apart."

Hock hesitated, "Yes sir."

"Invite the Targ to join in the kill."

"Yes sir."

Hock turned to the communications officer who was standing by and nodded. The young officer headed for the comm station to relay the message.

It was over Hock thought. All his fears had been for nothing. In the end, all the Admiral's strategizing couldn't surpass good old fashioned politics. Spivey had arranged for most of the Kardon fleet to turn away from the Admiral and that was what had won the day.

Now it appeared as if the Admiral didn't know what to do. He himself would be dead now if it wasn't for the sacrifice of that brave Fighting Ship.

"The *Reach* is slowing sir."

Hock turned to the young officer manning the scanner console. "What?"

"He's slowing, slightly."

Before Hock could respond Spivey said, "Now we have him. Full power!"

Hock was ashamed that he was thrilled by these last moments. There was something satisfying in destroying one who had done so much damage to the Imperial Fighting Force over the years. As much as he respected and admired his foe, he hated him.

He could see that they were catching up to the *Reach*. It would not be long now. It looked as if the Targ would reach it first. Still, Hock felt uneasy. Something wasn't right.

"Sir."

"What is it Hock?" Spivey asked without looking away from the main vidscreen.

"Something is . . .ah perhaps we should hold some of the fleet back."

Spivey turned to Hock slowly. Every eye on the bridge was focused on this exchange. "We are about to destroy what's left of the Kardon fleet and I want every member of this Armada to own claim to that glory," he said in a raised voice.

The bridge crew cheered. Hock was properly chastised, and fortunate he wasn't executed on the spot for questioning a War Master's strategy during a battle. Yet, he didn't feel lucky. He felt uneasy.

The *Reach* was almost in weapons range. Suddenly the *Reach* put on a burst of speed driving straight for the Frontier. At that speed the transition layer to the Frontier space would be harder than plastisteel, Hock thought. The *Reach* would shatter into a fine mist.

It was obvious to Hock and everyone on the bridge of the *Viper* that the Admiral had decided to end the battle on his terms. He wouldn't let them have the satisfaction of the kill nor would he let himself be captured.

The *Reach* turned slightly at the last second and hit the Frontier at an oblique angle. It ricocheted off the shimmering wall of transition space and was shot out past the edge of the fleet.

Hock was stunned. Harmon had done the impossible. He must have put every ounce of power into his forward shields to have pulled off that maneuver. Now he was on the far side of both fleets with nothing in front of him but empty space. The entire Armada would have to slow and come about just to get into position to chase him.

"Slow to one half and prepare to come about!" barked Spivey in a tone that left no doubt as to his feelings on seeing such a reversal of fortune just before victory.

As the ship began to slow a laser bolt flashed past the main vidscreen. Two more passed by, both traveling in different directions. The ship rocked from several heavy blows.

"We're under attack Sir!" the scanning officer yelped.

"I know that!" Spivey spat. "Who's attacking us!?"

Escape Pod EP23405 FS Valiant

The noise in Captain Julie Bedford's mind was jumbled. Screams for help, explosions, voices talking to her saying things she couldn't recognize. There was only darkness, the noises and weightlessness. She thought she heard Pleat's voice through the din. Something about being in the next pod, then there was nothing.

She opened her eyes and they slowly adjusted to the dark. She was floating weightless in an escape pod. She knew instantly what had happened. Judging from the throb in her head she'd been knocked unconscious. Someone, probably Pleat, had thrown her into a pod and jettisoned it. Whoever it was didn't have time to strap her in.

She floated to the one small window of the pod to see what, if anything, could be learned about the *Valiant*. She saw flashes of laser bolts hitting the massed ships of the Vicassian Armada and the Targ.

As soon as she saw what was happening she knew what *had* happened. The Kardon fleet had maneuvered into a massive sphere encompassing the Vicassian and Targ ships which had been led to the edge of the Frontier by Admiral Harmon. The Kardon fleet was spread out just enough to make them harder targets while still being able to mass their fire power.

The Vicassian effort to extricate itself from the trap made matters worse. Their ships turned without any order and many were in the unfortunate position of being pointed away from the enemy toward the interior of the Armada. The ships in the center of the formation could not fire.

Harmon had used the Frontier to leverage the punch of his much smaller fleet. He also brought easy victory to many who would not have stayed for a long fight. Now they were raining laser bolts down on a confused and paralyzed enemy.

Julie could see many ships jockeying to form a counter attack but the ships already out of action were hampering their efforts. The longer it took, the more disabled craft piled up at the outer edges of the Armada.

Bright red explosions were peppered throughout the mass of jiggling ships. Julie knew they were caused by the Lancet torpedoes. She also knew there were plenty more already on the way.

SS Viper, Command Ship of the first Imperial Fleet (IFF 1)

Hock could see that nearly every light on every console was lit. Noise from claxons, officers screaming orders into their comm stations and smoke filled the air. Spivey was in a rage. He'd been bested and he knew it.

It was the Salt Nebulae all over again Hock thought. The Admiral used cunning to defeat a stronger and presumably wiser foe. He'd sucked them into the very trap they were laying for him and the Kardon fleet. It's a good bet he'd brought enough torpedoes and such to finish the job.

Spivey appeared through the smoke, his red eyes blazing. "Hock you fat idiot don't just stand there, get over to tactical and ascertain our options."

"Yes sir!" Hock yelled over the din and headed toward the tactical station. When he got there he discovered a young officer slumped over the console. The boy was dead. He'd been killed when the console overloaded and exploded.

Hock moved to the nearby scanner station which was empty. He checked the relative positions of all the warring ships. The Kardon fleet formed a sphere that enveloped the entire Armada including the Targ contingent. The only portion not covered was that which was pressed against the Frontier itself.

The Kardon fleet was hammering them from all sides. If they shrank the sphere there would be no escape for anyone. Hock could see from the damage already sustained by the Armada there was very little time left to mount a counter attack.

The ship rolled violently. Every light on the bridge blinked once then went out. Decompression explosions rocked the ship as the massive Maxell armor plating was ripped from the ship's superstructure.

Hock knew the sounds he'd just heard were not the result of enemy weapons. They were the sounds made when two ships collided. Now it seems their panicked commanders were as great a danger as the Kardon. Perhaps more so.

"Hock!," Spivey bellowed over the noise and confusion, "Get to the nearest comm station and order all ships full stop!"

"Yes, sir!"

Command Ship Reach (C.S. 401k)

"Sir, the Vicassian fleet has stopped moving and we are being hailed by the *SS Viper*."

"Signal all ships to cease fire."

"But sir, you ordered that they disable their comm systems."

"Yes, the commanders now know why. It's a good bet they've reestablished comm contact. Send the message. Send it via flash also."

Plex was immediately at his side. "Sir, if we break off the fight now it may give them the opportunity to organize a counterattack."

Zach watched as the laser bolts from the fleet tapered off and the last Lancet Torpedo hit home. He took a deep breath. "We've won Plex. There is no need for me to destroy the lives of those crewmen. They serve their fighting force as we do ours. This war has already taken enough lives."

"Yes Sir," Plex said dejectedly. He wanted to see the Vicassian Armada, the majority of which was already in pieces heading for the Frontier, crushed beyond recognition. He was also a little ashamed of himself for wanting so much death for crewman he'd never met.

"Pleat!"

"Sir."

"We've got work to do."

From: Dr. Flubdubulous [mailto:DrF@napkin.com]
Sent: Monday, November 1, 2004 9:01 AM
To: Bruce Bauries Euphoria Pictures
Subject: Blood, Death, and Sky!

Due to the recent changeover by a major motion picture studio to Blue-Ray from HD, I've shutdown production on Euphoria East's production of "Blood, Death and Sky: The Pennsylvania Edition." The original footage was shot on a handy cam and a cell phone camera and I am concerned that the end product may not be up to date when finished. There were other technical problems however. In an homage to Stephen Spielberg and Ingmar Bergman, I decided to add a scene wherein Death, dressed in a clown suit, watches disinterestedly as dinosaurs attack a group of homeless men. Since I didn't have a stop-motion camera I had to dress up several pit bulls as dinosaurs. In retrospect, it is easy to conclude that rubbing the homeless men with raw meat just before shooting was a mistake but one could easily argue that tragedies occur on all movie sets and it was just an unfortunate coincidence that the dog wrangler was on a beer-run when the mishap occurred. Fortunately, a little known codicil in the Patriot Act removed all lawful rights from the homeless so there won't be any legal costs to strain the budget. I shall keep you apprised of my progress.

PS No beer was wasted during the making of this film.

From: Daily Star Feedback
[mailto:dlystrfdbk@broadstream.net]
Sent: Monday, November 1, 2004 10:25 AM
To: Dr. Flubdubulous
Subject: FW: FEEDBACK

Funny, Funny, Funny!\

*****

Enough with the turtle. It stopped being funny six columns ago.

*****

I'd love to know where you get your brilliant ideas. Please do a column on that.

*****

Please stop writing. You suck!

*****

You are a Bumble Bee. Bumble Bees sometimes get swatted.

*****

My son and I read your column religiously. We'd love to meet you. Will you be doing any public appearances?

*****

I AM trying to kill you and I WILL succeed.

Sincerely,

Spivey

*****

If the turtle is so bad why don't you just hire a dolphin to kick the shit out of it?

*****

PENNSYLVANIA FISH AND GAME COMMSSION

XX XXXXX XXXXXX
XXXXX
XXXXXXXX XXXX

Dear Sir,

It has come to our attention that you have featured in your column an intention to kill a box turtle which you feel is trying to kill you. We believe your attention to this subject is almost certainly a matter of artistic license and not based on any real intent to kill a common box turtle, however, in the off chance you may be serious, we would like to take this time to remind you that the animal, Terrapine Carolinas, is an endangered species and therefore protected from hunting.

Sincerely,

XXXXXXX XXXXXXXXX

PS You should know we have received several thousand calls of complaints from concerned citizens who believe you intend to harm the turtle in question.

THE HUMANE SOCIETY

XXX XXXX XXXXX
XXXXX XXXXX
XXXX XX, XXXXXX

Dear Sir,

We here at the humane society have read your recent columns with increasing concern.

We believe your attempts at humor concerning the killing of a turtle might induce your readers to do the same. Unfortunately, we live in a society that is heavily influenced by media. It is incumbent upon the media to control itself. This is a heavy responsibility indeed. Accordingly, we must ask that you please refrain from making any future reference to killing any animals. Thank you.

Sincerely,

XXXX XXXXXXXXX

Dear Mr. Flubdubulous,

We do not have dogs trained to hunt turtles. People don't hunt turtles. Sorry.

XXXX XXXXXXX

Dear Dr. Flubdubulous,

I am an independent film maker and I would like to film you and your struggle against Spivey. You can check my film credits on IMDB. Please contact me at your earliest convenience. Thank you.

Lance W. Beeks

Home XXX-XXX-XXXX

Cell XXX-XXX-XXXX

Dr. F.

    We would like to help you catch Spivey to show all the bleeding hearts that man has dominion over the animals like the Bible says. Just let us know where you live and I and my friends will be there pronto with our shotguns.

Yours Truly

XXXXX XXXXXXXX

Chapter Ten

Daily Star-Home and Leisure Section D-*November 7, 2004*

Regrets

I knew a woman who told me that she had absolutely no regrets. It was an extraordinary thing for me to hear. I kind of felt she said it just a little too vehemently which made me think she was trying to convince herself as much as me. Nevertheless, as one who is filled with regrets, I was flabbergasted.

Over the years, in the quiet moments, I would try to imagine what it would be like to live a life with absolutely no regrets. To have had the good fortune, the skill, the talent to do nothing one regrets.

I have accumulated so many regrets, so much borne of shame and stupidity you could set out to put each next to a star in the night sky and you would run out of stars before you were done.

My greatest regret was that I didn't enjoy the people in my life. I should have cherished my every moment with them but instead I got caught up in everything else. I focused on stupid things.

Someone said that a statement that can never be false in any way, is worthless. So I'll choose my words here carefully. Some say character is destiny. That may be true but I've come to believe that you choose your reality and thus your perception of destiny.

I have endured a great deal of criticism from religious people because I've dared to ask questions and think-plus I thought I was a god for a time. I've also come under criticism because I've always doubted those who presumed to speak for the almighty.

I started to wonder what would happen if God spoke for herself? What if you could have a two way conversation with the man himself? What do you think you'd say? Perhaps that is a conversation nobody would want. That's one bucket of cold water nobody wants splashed on their perceptions I'll wager.

I think I know how my conversation would go and I'm ashamed. I'll share it with you anyway.

I'm sure it would start with pleasantries. I assume God has impeccable manners. Then I would say something like, "So what's the deal, did I do well with my life?" God would have the answer immediately of course but he'd pause just to be polite. Then he'd say, "It's not about that. It's about others. You enrich yourself when you enrich their lives. You serve me when you serve others.

"I gave you a beautiful world with beautiful people and all you did was ignore the beauty that surrounded you. You chased after material wealth, conflict with others, and methods of personal destruction."

At this point, God would pause, much like a kindly camp counselor or old friend of the family. She'd probably put a hand on my shoulder. Then get back to it. He'd say, "I love you and the people you quarreled with, without end. I cherished you the way you could have and should have cherished your loved ones."

I'd know she would be right on the money and I might even hang my head. Thinking about all that had been said. Secretly hoping it was over.

Then He'd hit me with the big guns. She'd say, You know what bothered me most?" I'd have to ask even though the answer would be the last thing I'd want to know. "You never took care of you. You never let yourself be as nice as you could be to others. You never allowed yourself to forgive those whom you perceived wronged you and thus you carried around a great deal of anguish. When you hurt you, you hurt me and all those who loved you."

No doubt, at that point, God would probably smile partly because He was intimating that She forgave me and perhaps a little of the smile would be directed at the absurdity which is the number of people to whom the aforementioned remarks pertain to.

As far as I'm concerned, it was my sole ambition these last few years to create a little beauty for a weary world before the Grim Reaper, already hot on my heels, caught up with me. I regret that I failed to do so.

The Sioux have a saying, "Count no man lucky until he has had a good death."

My Dearest Polly

In answer to your last letter, I'm sorry but I don't have any photographs of myself when I was young. We didn't have much money and even if we had, I'm sure my parents would have spent it on mental health services for your Uncle Tom.

As you know I grew up on Long Island, met your mother there, married her, then moved out here. Somewhere in between I had car accidents, barbeques, went to college, learned sign language so that I could raise you and learned the secret to life (I'll tell you when you're older). However, for some reason, I didn't take many photographs during those times.

I'm sorry if my decision to stand up to Spivey upsets you. However, I can assure you that my decision is not as irrational as some have claimed. You may already be learning at your fancy-pants college that not everything is as it seems.

I cannot predict the outcome of what must happen in the near future but you should know that you and your sister (and to a lesser extent, your mother) were the joys of my life. I was only alive while with you, the rest was wasted.

ALL my love

Daddy

REDEMPTION

By Dr. Flubdubulous

PART 7

Command Ship Reach (C.S. 401k)

Admiral Zach Harmon was stuffing the last of his gear into a small shoulder bag. Most of it had already been packed and sent to his mother's house. He zipped the bag and took a long look at the opulent quarters he'd spent so little time in these past few months.

The door chimed. "Come in Plex."

The door slid open and Plex stepped in wearing the standard black on black uniform of the Suh-vak except that now he had the insignia of a full Colonel on his collar.

"How'd you know it was me?"

"I didn't, I've been saying that all morning. I figured sooner or later I'd be right."

Plex smiled briefly not entirely sure his old friend was joking with him. Zach had seemed almost psychic during the now famous Second Battle of the Frontier and his actions during these past two cycles only enhanced his legend.

"So you're really doing it?"

"Yes Sir, Colonel Sir."

"You can't do this."

Zach stopped packing and looked at his old friend carefully for a moment. "Plex, I've spent my entire life in the service of the Space Force. I think it's time for a little break."

"But the Space Force needs you. They made you a full Admiral and awarded you the Platinum Star. You're in line to be the Space Commander some day. You're gonna throw all that away to explore the Frontier looking for people who are more than likely already dead?"

Breathing hard, his face flushed, the words came out in a rush and Plex was only slightly less ashamed than he was frustrated. His face felt hot.

Zach reached out and put a hand on Plex's shoulder. "Plex, I know you are concerned for me but you're wrong about the Space Force. There are many who did not wish for us to succeed against the Armada. They fear retribution now that we were victorious despite their efforts. There are many who are angry that I agreed to accept an armistice instead of destroying every last Vicassian and Targ at the Frontier."

"The Suh-vak will find the traitors and you can handle the rest. You've got a hell of a lot of support within the Space Force. There are many who owe their lives to you."

"Yes, and as much as they owe me, I owe the crew of the *Valiant* whom I may yet be able to save. Let's not forget who bought and paid for that shiny Platinum Star that graces my trophy case."

"People die in battle. They knew the risks and they gladly accepted them."

"Easy Plex, I don't know about the 'gladly' part. But they saved my life and I intend to return the favor if I can."

"So you're going to abandon Kardon and the Space Force when they need you most?"

"Plex, I was serious when I told you before the battle that I was afraid of the consequences of our winning."

"So why'd you-"

"Win?" Zach chuckled, "What choice did I have? But the war is over, Kardon is safe." He paused, "Until the next one anyway. I'm not in the business of fixing political systems and societies."

"So you're turning your back on that?"

"I'm not turning my back on the crew of the *Valiant*. Plex, I've come to believe that the only thing that really matters are our loved ones, the rest is . . . the rest, and not nearly as important."

"You could search the Frontier for ten life times and never find a one of them."

Zach smiled slowly. "Yes, now give me a kiss goodbye old friend." Zach kissed Plex on the lips then hugged him. Plex, with tears in his eyes, turned and left.

Zach finished packing and went to visit his ready room for one last time before departing. It was almost completely dark as he preferred. It didn't make sense but he felt he thought better in the half light. Keeping the lighting to a minimum also made best use of the giant viewport.

Standing at the viewport Zach could see much of his fleet had already departed and many more were going back out on patrol. Their movements didn't look as ominous as before the battle and he didn't feel as heavy. He didn't turn when the door slid open.

Zach knew it was Pleat. He didn't know how he knew but he did. Perhaps it was the way that the door slid open when Pleat was the one who activated it. The old Ensign refused retirement so long as Zach was still Admiral.

"Sir."

"As of today it's Zach, Pleat. And please don't tell me the Vicassians have formed another Armada and are looking to get even."

"No Sir. It's a Captain Bedford to see you sir."

Now Zach turned to search Pleat's face. Blank as usual. The name was familiar but this past cycle of celebrations and more celebrations was full of names. Everyone wanted a minute with him.

"I'm not in the mood for a vidsession with another ambitious captain. Please make my excuses."

"Yes sir, but I think you should see her."

Zach studied Pleat's face for a long moment. Again, he could read nothing from the blank countenance.

"Very well, send her in but if this is another vidsession I'm going to have you executed as my final act as Admiral."

"Yes Sir."

Pleat went to the door. When it slid open there was a woman standing in the hall. Pleat motioned for her to enter. He slipped out just after she stepped into the room. She hesitated by the door.

She could see the Admiral standing on the wide platform in front of the largest viewport she'd ever seen. He was tall, lean, and looked very much like he did in the countless newsvids she'd seen of him.

"You're out of uniform Captain."

"Huh?" Julie looked down at her clothes. She climbed the steps to the platform and saluted Zach. He returned her salute with the enthusiasm of a cadet on the first day of training which made her feel even more out of uniform.

"Sir, I'm no longer a member of the Space Force."

"Then why am I talking to you and why are you calling yourself Captain?"

"I am Captain Bedford, . . . I was Captain of the *Valiant*."

Zach inhaled deeply in an almost autonomic response at the mention of the *Valiant*. His reaction surprised him as much as it did her. Now he remembered the name. He'd received a report that she had survived the battle. There was talk of court martial for Captain Bedford until Zach talked to the Star Commander himself about the matter.

"She was a good ship with a great crew," Zach said without changing the expression on his face.

"Thank you Admiral. I'd like to thank you also for interceding with the Star Commander on my behalf."

"No thanks is necessary," he said and began to turn away in the time tested method of senior officers had for ending a conversation with a subordinate.

"I didn't just come here for that," she said more harshly than she wanted to.

Zach turned back to face her again. "Oh?"

"Yes, Sir, I've come because I know what you are planning next and I want to be a part of it."

Zach raised his eyebrows as if to say, 'go on.'

"You're going to search for the crew of the *Valiant* in the Frontier and I want to go with you."

"How did you come to that conclusion?"

"I know you were offered this ship as a trophy for destroying the Vicassians yet you chose a pre-war mine sweeper. I know you had it refitted with the latest reactors, weapons and scanning equipment."

"Captain, my first assignment was aboard a mine sweeper. It was out of nostalgia that I chose one for my personal ship. They also require a smaller crew compliment to operate."

"I think you chose it because it is sturdier than any other ship in the fleet, this one included. You'd need such a ship to weather the Frontier."

"Well," he looked over at the chronometer on the wall near the door, "in a little while I'll be a citizen again, free to go where I choose and as much as I would like to include you in my crew-"

"I saved your life" she blurted out and grabbed him by the arm.

Zach put his hand on hers and said quietly, "I know and I thank you."

"Then take me with you," she said, the desperation in her voice rising.

"Well-"

"They meant as much to me as they did to you. If you were in my shoes wouldn't you be dying to go?"

He couldn't argue with her last point. Zach knew she was right but he also knew she'd be throwing away her career. But then, who was he to judge on that issue.

"I'm not saying that I am going to the Frontier, but you may join my crew as my Executive Officer."

She felt instant relief at his offer. She looked down and realized that she was still gripping his arm. She couldn't let go even though she knew she should. All the emotion of losing her ship, leaving the Space Force and finding a way to search for the crew of the *Valiant* came rushing at her. She gripped his arm harder even though she wanted to stop this embarrassing display.

Zach could see the flood of emotion hitting her but could do nothing about it. He resolved to let her have her moment. Losing a ship is no small matter. Most captains preferred to stay with the ship no matter the consequences. That was something the *Valiant's* crew would hardly have tolerated. She was here now because of them.

After a short while he said, "Captain if you intend to claim me, don't you think you ought to speak with my mother first?"

"What?" She loosened her grip but didn't let go. "Oh yes, forgive me Admiral." She finally let her hand fall to her side.

She recovered quickly. She was intelligent but it was more likely she'd learned of his plans from Pleat. Plex was the only person he'd told and there's no way a Colonel in the Suhvak would tell a Captain in the Space Force anything. Old Pleat must have figured out what he was planning and informed her, Zach concluded.

They both started for the door.

"So, how many crewman do we have so far?"

"Beside you and I . . . zero."

-----Original Message-----

From: Dr. Flubdubulous [mailto:DrF@napkin.net]
Sent: Sunday, November 8, 2004 3:03 AM
To: Tom Anderson
Subject: Character is Destiny

Following excerpt was taken from the personal journal of Admiral Flubdubulous, written just before the now famous Battle of Spivey.

It is the hour before dawn and were I the favored son of the muses, it would still be beyond my pen to describe my apprehension at this time. I know the enemy and battle, is near. I can only hope that when the sun rises a fair wind shall rise with it and pray that heaven not be blinded to the evil nature of my foe. For his vile and disreputable conscience would in no way impede his most vicious ambition which history will attest is without border and unknown to decency.

Soon I must wake my men to see perhaps their last sunrise. I am confident however that providence shall not permit their lives to be sacrificed in vain. Victory shall smile upon their broken bodies and honor will write their history. For the best efforts of my malevolent adversary cannot molest their memory.

WE SAIL INTO HISTORY!

Goodbye,

-----Original Message-----
From: Dr. Flubdubulous [mailto:DrF@napkin.net]
Sent: Sunday, November 8, 2004 3:45 AM
To: Reverend Hummel
Subject: Character is Destiny

Dear Reverend,

Permit me to explain my position in your terms. "As a man thinks in his heart, so is he." (Proverbs 23:7). I dislike you because in your heart you are a scared fool who turns his fears into aggression towards others. You hide your aggression behind a veneer of piety because here too you lack the courage to state that your goal is to dominate others. You would gladly sacrifice free speech and independent thought and all the benefits they bring in order to satiate your insatiable desire to control.

It's true I lost my mind about a year ago but you should know that even crazy people have ambition. Mine is to bring a little happiness to a weary world before the grim reaper, already hot on my heels, catches up with me.

You frequently state your love for the Lord however, I would point out to you that "he that fears is not made complete in love." (1 John 4:18). You need to identify, confront and cast out your fears. Only then can you truly posses the love for the Lord and your fellow man that you profess.

I do wish you luck however.

Dr. F.

Dolly,

All the granite castles I built in my mind had, in reality, no more substance than swirling smoke. What I thought was real was not so. That which I thought was permanent was ephemeral. My love for you has sustained me throughout our time together. Yet, that love for all its worth, cannot relieve me of my mortality and it's one attendant obligation.

The worst part of this past year has been my inability to meet the needs of you and the girls. And, as hard as it is to understand, what I do next I do for you and the girls.

I don't know if there is an afterlife,
however, if there is, you can be certain, I'll
love you there too.

All my love

> -----Original Message-----
From: Dr. Flubdubulous   [mailto:DrF@napkin.net]
Sent: Sunday, November 8, 2004 4:13 AM
To: Bruce Bauries Euphoria Pictures
Subject: Goodbye

I am sorry to inform you that I must now end
our relationship. You may send any and all
monies due me to my wife, Dolly Anderson.

Best,

Dr. F.

PS I'm sorry you never sent me the money you
promised me. I cannot make you a better
person. But if I could . . . Man!, you would
be great! Take care of yourself.

Dr. F. Found Dead

By Dennis Pick

The Associated Press

Dr. Flubdubulous, formerly Andrew J. Anderson, was found dead on his small farm in central Pennsylvania today.

Dr. Flubdubulous, a writer, was best known for his eccentric viewpoints. He developed a cult following but was most famous for his contention that he was being stalked by a box turtle. He once stated that he had geared his work toward alien sensibilities since he believed they made up the majority of his fan base. His human fans referred to themselves as Flub-heads and frequently meet to debate the topics featured in the Dr.'s writings.

Dr. Flubdubulous, age 43, was found by two hunters crossing his property. Investigators do not suspect foul play and, they stated, no turtles were found in the area.

Obituaries

Andrew J. Anderson 43

METROVILLE - Mr. Anderson went to rest on November 8, 2004. He is survived by his wife Dolly and two daughters Polly and Molly.

Mr. Anderson graduated Cum Laude from Stony Brook University in 1982 with a degree in Accounting. He worked in the business department at Susquehanna College for fifteen years. He left Susquehanna to pursue a career as a writer and published his works under the pen name Dr. Flubdubulous.

In lieu of flowers, please consider a gift in Mr. Anderson's name to the Diabetes Fund.

Editor's Note: Dr. Flubdubulous was laid to rest on November 10th 2004. A cause of death was not determined. His headstone, by his request, contained only the following:

"Those whom the gods would destroy, they first make mad."

www.ingramcontent.com/pod-product-compliance
Lightning Source LLC
Chambersburg PA
CBHW022122080426
42734CB00006B/224

9 7 8 1 4 3 5 7 7 8 1 9 1